Heroes

in Our Midst

INSPIRATIONAL STORIES
FROM SINGLE MOMS

RALPH UJANO, JR,

Founder, Helping Hands for Single Moms Dallas

HEROES IN OUR MIDST – INSPIRATIONAL STORIES FROM SINGLE MOMS

Paperback ISBN: 978-1-953806-46-8
Ebook ISBN: 978-1-953806-47-5

First Published in the USA in 2020 by Spotlight Publishing™
Book Cover: Jim Aubele
Authors: Susan Sweet / Ralph Ujano, Jr.
Editor: Susan Sweet
Compiled by: Chris Coffman
Interior Design: Becky Norwood

For Information Contact:

Ralph Ujano, Jr
Helping Hands for Single Moms Dallas www.HelpingHandsforSingleMoms.org

Heroes

in Our Midst

INSPIRATIONAL STORIES
FROM SINGLE MOMS

RALPH UJANO, JR

Founder, Helping Hands for Single Moms Dallas

Spotlight PUBLISHING

Goodyear, AZ

TABLE OF CONTENTS

DEDICATION

For Ruben Salazar, the high school mentor that inspired my own journey to graduate college. Your legacy includes all our single mom college graduates and their families.

In loving memory of Gene Pope. As my uncle, he showed me the value of family and as a college professor, taught me that learning can be fun. His humor makes me smile to this day.

ENDORSEMENTS

"These inspiring stories of single mom college students determined to gain an education and financial independence for their families-against seemingly insurmountable obstacles-reaffirms my decision to help support the launch of Helping Hands for Single Moms Dallas."

~G. Brint Ryan,
Chairman and CEO of Ryan, LLC

"Heroes in Our Midst not only celebrates these {women}, but demonstrates what can happen when a call to serve, a vision to lead, and a helping hand divinely come together."

~Cynt Marshall,
CEO Dallas Mavericks

"Heartwarming, emboldening, encouraging, a lift to your soul and spirit! These testimonies shared by such resilient moms remind you that what seems impossible can be accomplished when willing hearts allow God to work His miracle through them."

~Janice Parker,
Golden Gate Missionary Baptist Church, Dallas, Texas

"As you read *Heroes in Our Midst*, you will find yourself rooting for these single moms to overcome the many obstacles they face. It is never too late for a new beginning."

~Lucille O'Neal,
Author, Motivational Speaker, and one of the founding members of the Mothers of Professional Basketball Players, Inc. (MPBP)

"In 2014 I fell in love with the Helping Hands for Single Moms organization (HHFSM); this book reminds me why."

~Eddie Johnson,
NBA veteran and co-host of NBA Today on Sirius XM NBA Radio

"You can't read *Heroes in Our Midst* without being challenged by these undeterred women who faced significant obstacles to creating a new life for themselves and their children. They remind us to pursue what is truly important in life."

~Dr. Norm Wakefield,
Professor Emeritus, Phoenix Seminary

"Nothing motivates my walk with God quite like inspiring stories of God's transforming grace to single moms rising to glory out of the ashes. Thank you for inspiring me. You are true heroes!"

~Dr. Charles Rasmussen,
Senior Pastor Community Church of Sun Village

SINGLE MOM -
YOU ARE A HERO!

You may not consider yourself one. You may have never been celebrated as such. In fact, the culture may be treating you much differently. In some circles, you feel as though you have failed and that you and your children are now a burden on society. Your potential has been stifled, your dreams will never be, and your only chance at redemption can be found in marriage and taking on the appearance of a "normal" family.

Do not let the opinions of others define you. True heroes are admired or idealized for courage, outstanding achievements, or noble qualities. You, the single mom, are a warrior standing in the gap to lead, nurture, and protect your children. You are, by definition, a hero.

Heroes in Our Midst was written for you. The women who share their stories want you to know that just as they were able to rise above their challenges, you can too. Through these pages, be inspired and reminded that:

- You are a hero.
- Look up. The Greatest Hero will give you wisdom and insight to lead well.
- People you don't even know believe in you. Organizations like **Helping Hands For Single Moms Dallas** are for you and exist to encourage you on your journey.

- Every mom in this book thought at one time that she was no one special, just another of society's single moms. Learn from and be encouraged by the power fierce love has to change a mom's life for the sake of her children.

To all moms, dads, siblings, friends, and pastors of single moms: *Heroes in Our Midst* is a book of inspiration not only for these moms but for those who love them. We encourage you to pass along a copy of the book to the single mom in your life, slip a "You Are My Hero" letter in the front cover, and give these everyday heroes the recognition they deserve.

Cynt Marshall
CEO of the Dallas Mavericks

FOREWORD

I understand single motherhood. I witnessed the sacrifices of motherhood. I was shaped by the tired hands of a wonderful mother.

It was the summer of 1975, I was 15 years old, my father broke my nose when I stepped in to protect my mom from his physical abuse that had gone on for years. He was violently angry because my mom left him and moved us to a safe environment. She took her children, a purse, and a Bible.

My mom is my hero. She worked two to three jobs to take care of us. She sometimes went to bed hungry after she made sure we were fed. My mom often visited our schools and attended our events, even while working. I still don't know how she did it. She understood teenagers and helped us six kids through many problems, wiping many tears away. We came first. Our physical and emotional well-being was always top of mind. And that is still the case.

My mom spent a lot of time with her children, playing games, watching TV, going to church, attending events, and eating dinner together (without my father). She did all of this while enduring years of violence and regular beatings. Although there are things she will never tell us, I saw enough to know that she often felt pain while determined to experience the joys of motherhood.

My mom gave me the foundation for a good life – a math book and a Bible! She showed me how to overcome adversity with grace and forgiveness. She taught me the value of hard work. My mom is a role model of what it takes to be a great mother. She is my role model. Mom is my hero. I am proud to be the daughter of Carolyn Gardner and in her honor, I submit the foreword for *Heroes in Our Midst*.

This literary work is more than a book. It is a collection of life's term papers from graduates of the **Helping Hands for Single Moms** (HHFSM) program. Many of the stories on these pages remind me of my mother. Grit and grace. Faith and family. Resilience and results. I am delighted to use my voice to amplify these remarkable stories.

Like the women who will touch you as the pages unfold, my mom was and remains a strong woman of faith. She showed us the love of Christ and led us to Him. She believes in the power of prayer and taught her children how to pray. She taught us that with God all things are possible. She passed on the love of the scriptures to us and taught us to hide ourselves in God's word.

True to the mission of HHFSM, my mother's hands can still be found helping others, especially mothers who are struggling to provide for their children. Always believing in the power of education, my mother epitomizes the mission to serve low-income single mom college students. *Heroes in Our Midst* not only celebrates these students but demonstrates what can happen when a call to serve, a vision to lead, and a helping hand divinely come together.

I love the HHFSM organization. My support of their programs will continue to represent my wonderful mother, Carolyn Gardner, and her legacy of sacrifice and lending a helping hand.

Cynt Marshall

INTRODUCTION

by
Chris Coffman

The Helping Hands for Single Moms Story

I wasn't raised by a single mom, nor did I marry one. I also don't have a sibling or close relative who endured the challenges of single motherhood. To be honest, I never gave much thought to the struggles of single moms - those incredible "heroes in our midst," until one hot summer morning in Phoenix, Arizona, in 2001.

As a member of a ministerial alliance group looking for our next community project, I was assigned the mission of driving through a specific section of the city to observe the various needs of people in our neighborhoods. That day, my search began with a short prayer that was answered within five minutes, when I noticed a young, four-year-old boy walking unattended on the busy street I was driving. My quest gave way to the alarming concern and warning lights within my mind of the danger this very young boy faced being out on this major thoroughfare all alone. I immediately pulled over, rolled down my window, and announced to the young man that he needed to meet me on the corner so that I could walk him home. At that moment, another caring woman who had made the same observation pulled up and joined us.

Surprisingly, this young adventurer knew where he lived and led us back into his neighborhood to an old, dilapidated house. I knocked and waited. The door slowly cracked and the face of a young girl, perhaps nine to ten years old, peered out. Upon seeing her brother with two strangers, the girl's eyes grew wide, and her mouth dropped open. She knew this wasn't good. I asked, "Is this your brother, and are you supposed to be watching him?"

"Yes," she sheepishly replied. My next question would change the course of my life when I asked to speak with her mom or dad. "Only my mom lives here," replied the young girl. She was the daughter of a single parent, trying to shoulder some of the household responsibilities to ease her mother's burden.

As we watched the boy safely retreat into the house and walked back to our vehicles, my mind was lost in thought. From that moment, I knew in my heart and in my mind that God's plan for me was to help single moms. That wandering young boy and his young sister helped me realize the plight of single mothers, and the impact or consequences that their situations can have on their children.

A short time later, with additional support and guidance, Helping Hands for Single Moms took shape. We defined our mission: to assist low- income single mom families while the mother pursues a post-secondary education, financial independence, and a positive family legacy. That serendipitous 2001 encounter with a little boy has resulted in an ever- expanding scholarship program that to date has provided over $6 million in scholarships and supportive services to hundreds of low-income single mom college student families.

The single-parent household is often a difficult reality for a married parent to comprehend. Married couples, to varying degrees, work together to manage the seemingly endless tasks of caring for their children. In a healthy marriage, a parent doesn't have to wonder who will back them up; who will give them a much-needed break; who will encourage them when parenting gets tough. When parenting is done in tandem, neither Mom nor Dad have to carry the sole burden of daily responsibilities such as getting the kids up and off to school; going to work all day; coming home to make dinner, run errands, put the kids to bed and complete an endless list of chores in the few hours before the day begins again. The two-parent family has a better chance of working through the common challenges that life brings forth such as illness, car problems, and conflicts in the kids' schedules. But for the single mom, any one of these hiccups can bring life to a devastating standstill.

This book is about just a few of the incredible women we have been blessed to serve during their journeys to make a better life for themselves and their children. These true-life stories highlight the fortitude, endurance, and strength to do what was needed, whenever it was needed in each of these women's circumstances. The challenges these moms faced could only be overcome by their unwavering commitment to be the mother they wanted for their children, bolstered by faith in something greater than themselves. These are the accounts of eight heroes in our midst, whom we had the privilege to assist through **Helping Hands for Single Moms**.

Sylvia's Story

1

THE MOM WHO INSPIRED HELPING HANDS FOR SINGLE MOMS

W*hat would you need in order to go back to school right now?"*

Sylvia wasn't used to being asked what SHE needed.

Her whole life she had been the one taking care of everyone else. Yet through an unexpected chain of events, she found herself at this moment, seated in an unfamiliar church office, beside a social worker she had come to know and trust, fielding questions asked by a pastor she had never before met.

Sylvia wondered why complete strangers would want to help her. After all, she was just a Hispanic American woman with an unremarkable story.

Sylvia's stepdad married her single mom when Sylvia was two years old and her sister, Ruby, was still a baby. The family lived in a small farming community in Arizona where both parents worked long days in the fields. Soon a baby brother and later a little sister were added to their numbers. From kindergarten on, Sylvia was often responsible for the children. She was coached on what she must do to keep the little ones safe and her parents out of trouble for leaving her in charge until six or eight at night.

There was no answering the door, no playing with the other kids outside… even looking out the window was forbidden. When school was in session, Sylvia enjoyed getting out of the house and playing the role of a child her own age. But by first grade, Sylvia and Ruby were often pulled out of school to work in the potato fields alongside their parents. Schoolwork had to be made up late into the night, friends were difficult to make and keep, but Sylvia did her best to keep up and obey the rules at both school and home.

Sylvia missed her fourth-grade year entirely. Sylvia's stepdad moved the family to Mexico so that they could work on his family's ranch. School was a luxury the girls didn't need, and instead, they would learn life skills that no curriculum would ever cover. The family ranch was on a cotton field with acres and acres of work to be done. Sylvia picked cotton, took care of the goats and chickens, and washed the entire family's clothing by hand.

On a regular basis, Sylvia and Ruby were tasked with grinding the corn into masa for tortillas and tamales. It involved hours on end of hard labor using an antiquated grinder that took all their strength and left both of the girls exhausted. Life on the farm was not only hard on the kids. Sylvia's parents were having troubles of their own. About a year after the move, Sylvia's mom had enough, left her husband, and brought the kids back to the states.

Single and financially struggling, Sylvia's mom accepted her brother's offer of a temporary home. Per the familiar routine, the adults worked in the fields, but this time Sylvia had company as she and her oldest cousin took charge of their respective siblings. Sylvia was enrolled in the local school, assigned to the fourth-grade year she had missed while in Mexico. Word got out that Sylvia was a grade behind her age, and she was mercilessly teased by kids for being held back. One of Sylvia's teachers saw what was happening and took compassion on Sylvia. She knew Sylvia was a good student and a hard worker, so she appealed to the administration on Sylvia's behalf and got her moved up to the proper grade. She never forgot the kindness shown to her by a teacher who cared.

As the years went by, Sylvia had no choice but to forego what remained of her childhood and take life seriously. The tension in the household fluctuated as her stepdad came in and out of their lives. Moving from town to town to follow the work made connecting with kids and forming friendships nearly impossible. For Sylvia, every minute outside of school was spent raising her mother's kids... no school sports, no activities, no time to be a teenager. Sylvia only ever had one or two friends, and by late high school, she became involved with a boyfriend whom she met outside of school. The summer before her senior year, Sylvia found she was pregnant. That fall, she finished her high school credits, got married in November, and graduated that December.

In the spring, Sylvia gave birth to a beautiful daughter with whom she was able to stay home and be an actual mom. Tragically, two months after the baby was born, Sylvia's mother and youngest sibling were killed in a car accident involving a drunk driver. Sylvia would miss out once again on a rite of passage, having a mother to advise her and share in her joy as she raised a child of her own.

Married life began as a respite of sorts for Sylvia. Her husband had a steady job at the meat-processing plant, so, unlike fieldwork, the family could stay in one place and put down roots. Sylvia kept a clean home as she had always done for her mother and took great care of her daughter, and soon after, her son. Sylvia kept in close contact with her sister Ruby, who was also starting a family. As Sylvia's children grew, she took them to the local school and got involved with the Head Start program. It gave the children socialization and Sylvia was able to get out of the house and volunteer in the classroom. She loved being a part of the program, and it showed.

When the topic of returning to school was first presented to Sylvia, she gave it little consideration. The teachers at the program had suggested she look into college so that she could get paid as an employee since she was already volunteering so much of her time with Head Start. They knew she didn't have much and that she loved working

with the kids in the program. To the observer, it seemed a natural fit, but Sylvia was unsure of herself. Life for Sylvia was never about setting goals and raising expectations. It was more about finding a way to be content no matter the circumstances. She had watched her mom work hard labor her whole life, never having the security of a home base, all while juggling a rocky relationship and four kids. Aspirations were a luxury meant for other people. Sylvia's life was just fine at the moment, and she didn't want to rock that boat. Little did Sylvia know that things were about to change.

Sylvia's husband struggled with substance abuse. She knew that and accepted it. But by the time the children were five and three, his problems had expanded to infidelity. Sylvia protected her kids from their father's struggles as best she could, but eventually, his behaviors grew beyond her ability to make excuses and look the other way. In addition to the hurt he caused Sylvia by having an affair, she now had to figure out how to support her children, and herself, should the marriage crumble entirely. Sadly, it did. Sylvia took the kids and moved in with Ruby.

Despite the turmoil, Sylvia was following a path that would change her life for the better. While volunteering for Head Start, she met Lee, a social worker with the program that visited Sylvia's school once a month. Lee's role involved getting parents the support they needed to have successful families. Lee was also a member of a church lead by a pastor named Chris Coffman. The church community had a passion for helping single moms succeed. Impoverished single-parent households led by overburdened mothers were becoming increasingly prevalent in the surrounding neighborhoods.

The moms often juggled more than one low-paying job with no financial help from the father, all while trying to keep their kids fed, safe, and loved. A committee of mission-minded church members with hearts to serve this demographic were sent into the community to gather information and share solutions.

During one particular meeting, Lee approached the committee about a young mother of two children she had met through the Head Start program. This mother was in dire straits at the moment but there was something about her character, her commitment, that gave Lee the feeling that this mom would do whatever it took to succeed for the sake of her children. Lee observed that this woman was great with kids, generous with her time, and was a two-year college degree away from making a career out of what she was already doing, teaching children.

"We would like to help you go back to school so you can earn a livable wage and take care of yourself and your children. How can we help you do that?" Pastor Chris and Lee were genuinely interested, even eager to hear Sylvia's response.

The Helping Hands for Single Moms scholarship program was born that very day and designed in large part by Sylvia's answers. In addition to the obvious need for tuition help, Sylvia lacked a means of transportation. Pastor Chris put the word out Sunday morning that their new program could use a car, should anyone want to make a donation. After service, Chris was approached by in-town visitors who had a car they wanted to donate. A local auto repair shop offered their services to keep the car in working order. Sylvia did not have a computer, so one was provided, along with computer lessons so that Sylvia could navigate her schoolwork. Obstacles were being eliminated one by one. Now all Sylvia had to do was register for her first semester… and do the schoolwork.

Sylvia was anxious to get started on her new path. Since the divorce, Sylvia had found work in both fast food and daycare, but when a Head Start recruiter at her son's school discovered Sylvia was enrolled in college, he invited her to apply for a paid position, and she was hired. More than a job, Sylvia landed a career with stability, benefits, and opportunities for growth. One of the first things Sylvia did was apply for government-assisted housing and move her children from her sister's house to a place of her own.

As Sylvia completed class after class, a new confidence gave her the courage to finally dream about her future. She wondered if someday she could save enough to buy her own house. Around that time, Chris introduced Sylvia to Habitat for Humanity. He walked her through the application process, and eventually, she was approved. Near the end of her degree program, Sylvia was handed the keys to her very own house. Graduation was the icing on the cake.

Not only did Sylvia receive her Associate Degree in Early Childhood Education, she later went on to earn a Bachelor's Degree as well. She has worked for Head Start for nearly 20 years, doing what she loves most. To date, she has built into the lives of more than 400 young students, encouraging them to work hard and dream big. But her greatest impact has been on her own children. Her daughter Celli reflects on the mother she has come to admire:

> *"Mom is a true caretaker. She puts aside her own feelings, needs, and wants for the sake of those around her. When I was young and my parents split up, I didn't understand. I blamed my mom for the divorce. My dad would sometimes call and say he was coming to see me. I'd sit on the curb for hours watching for his car. He rarely kept his word. My mom would comfort me, buy me ice cream, and tell me she loved me. No matter how much I projected my anger on her, she never spoke against my father. It wasn't until I was much older that I discovered the truth behind their divorce. I was overcome with relief that it wasn't my fault, and guilt over blaming my mom. But true to her character, my mom was very forgiving.*

My mom wanted my brother and me to have the childhood she didn't. She did not involve us in any of the challenges she faced over the years, like divorce, financial problems, fear of making ends meet, and exhaustion. We knew she worked hard, but in our eyes, she had it all under control and we could keep on being kids.

Education was always a top priority. As we got older, Mom started telling us that we had to finish college before we could move out on our own. I began pursuing a business degree with plans to own and manage a hair salon. Along the way, I found I had an aptitude for accounting, so I changed my major. When I began my master's degree program, I was working 60 hours a week managing a salon franchise. Before completing my degree, I was offered an internship with the State Department of Administration. This was a greater opportunity than the career I had planned, so with my mom's encouragement, I took a risk, demoted myself at the salon, accepted the internship, and was offered a full-time position upon graduation.

As a child of a single mom that pursued a college degree, I can speak to mothers who may worry about balancing parenting, work, and school. While your children may not understand at the time, they will, and they'll admire you for it. Talk to them along the way about what you are doing and why. Plant the seeds early that college is an achievable goal and one you hope they someday embrace."

Layla's Story

2

REFUSE TO LET YOUR PAST
DEFINE YOU

Layla would not allow her past to define her future. As she held her newborn daughter in her arms, she knew it was not too late to make some drastic changes... to start fresh. Layla loved her two little boys. She was a good mom to them and an amicable ex-wife to their father, with whom she shared custody. But this newborn was instantly different. This baby's father was not a good or kind man. Layla had not, nor would she ever marry him. The raising of this child would be all on Layla.

Layla's daughter deserved a strong female role model. Through tears, Layla realized that over the past year, her strength had diminished, her will had been watered down, and her actions were reactions to someone more powerful than herself. Layla barely recognized the person she had become. She resembled an abused woman she once knew and had vowed never to become. She resembled her mother.

Layla always thought of her childhood as "happy." She grew up with a mom and a dad, and a younger sister. Her parents were hard-working convenience store owners. Her grandparents lived close by and were an active part of her life. Grandma brought Layla to church and taught her that "in all things, God works for the good of those who love Him." She cherished every moment spent with her grandma.

Layla was a mix of ethnicities. Her father was from Iran, and her mother was of Mexican descent. There were conflicts in the marriage, each blaming the other's faults on their ethnic stereotypes. Layla didn't give her heritage much thought until her teenage years when she was sent to a different high school than most of her friends from childhood. She had a difficult time finding acceptance among her new peers. Because of her looks, she was "not Hispanic enough" to hang with the Hispanic kids and neither "Persian nor white enough" to fit in with the rest. She now viewed her mixed-race as carrying more weight than she had ever realized and became increasingly self-conscious. Her self-esteem took a big hit, her grades dropped, and she began to lower the high-achieving bar she had set for herself. By the time Layla started community college, she was swept up in an apathetic lifestyle surrounded by friends who likewise lacked a sense of purpose or direction.

There were problems brewing at home. Layla's father had always been strong, vocal, emotional, and domineering, especially when he argued with her mother. His words could be cruel. Layla just accepted her family's dynamics as normal. As Layla got older and spent more time out of the house with school and friends, she realized the unhealthy environment her home had become. She also noticed a change in her mom. Her mother seemed to have lost her spark. It was as if she had succumbed to the accusations, the criticism, the verbal lashings. This broke Layla's heart and drove a wedge between her and her father.

At 19, halfway through her sophomore year of college, Layla found out she was pregnant. The father of her child was a former high school classmate with whom she had re-connected. They had been friends at first, but the relationship evolved. Like most of their peers, neither took life too seriously nor had any intentions of making more of their dating relationship than what it was. The pregnancy was about to change all of that. Layla dreaded telling her parents the news. Gravely disappointed and embarrassed, Layla's mother demanded that they marry immediately. A date was set, Layla withdrew from college, and she exchanged wedding vows before her second trimester.

Soon, these two kids were raising a child of their own. They were unprepared for the new responsibilities of marriage and parenting. Their relationship suffered, but they both loved their son and persevered. When the second child came along, Layla watched with some regret as her former classmates prepared for college graduation. Layla had always assumed she would be a college graduate with a diploma and a career. But here she was, surrounded by diapers and baby bottles, picking up work hours in her parents' convenience store, trapped in a marriage based on circumstance rather than love.

The bright spot was motherhood. She loved these baby boys passionately. For them, she could endure the monotony, the disappointment, the regret of a life that was passing her by. But her husband could not.

Like Layla, her husband resented the life in which he found himself. He was too young to be the head of a household. He felt trapped and wanted out. Also, like Layla, he loved his boys, but he began to wonder what it would look like to be a dad but not a husband. They had been friends for so many years, but lasting love had not materialized. Irritated constantly by one another, the small house with two babies was chaos. Layla's husband grew more hostile towards her. He said things that hurt. He avoided coming home and stayed out with friends. He shut Layla out of their finances. He drank more and more. There was talk of divorce. Eventually, he moved in with his parents while he and Layla thought things through. Then one night, everything changed.

The color drained from Layla's face as she listened to the alarm in her friend's voice coming through the other end of the phone. "Your husband just showed up. Apparently, he's been drinking all day, and he's putting the boys' shoes on. He is determined to get behind the wheel and drive them back to his place. I'm trying to stop him, but he won't listen!"

Layla was at work and had asked her best friend to stay with her kids. She could picture the scene as her friend tried frantically to reason with Layla's husband whom she could hear in the background of the phone call. She felt so helpless knowing her husband was, at that very moment, putting their toddlers in the back of his car, no car seats, no voice of reason breaking through his foggy thinking. Layla knew that in his right mind, he would do anything to protect his sons. That was the problem. The alcohol had been clouding his thinking with increasing regularity. He was a good dad in a bad spot. At that moment, Layla knew she had to think fast... for all of them.

With the next phone call, Layla ended her marriage but saved her family. The police spotted her husband's car en route to his home. When they determined his level of intoxication and saw the kids in the vehicle, they threw the book at him. His license was suspended. He was sentenced and convicted of aggravated DUI. The authorities assured Layla that she did the right thing, but it didn't feel like it. Her husband - her boys' father

- now had a police record. Her phone call had been the nail in the coffin of her marriage.

She had become a single mom overnight, and the marriage born out of the embarrassment and shame of her family was undone. Layla was once again an unwed mother and, therefore a disgrace to her father. "You now have two strikes against you, Layla," her father told her, "You have children, and now you're divorced!" Layla's shame was immense.

Layla couldn't shut out her own accusing mental list of failures. Single mom, unemployed, college dropout, failed wife, a shame to her parents... Layla's self-esteem was at an all-time low. She still had two little lives to provide for and protect. She had to find a way. She applied for work at convenience stores, the mall, gas stations... all without a single returned phone call. The desperation clouded her judgment just in time for a new man to walk into her life.

He was charming at first. He worked hard and took an interest in her boys. He wasn't put off by the fact that Layla was a package deal with kids in tow. He seemed to intuitively know all that Layla was lacking at that moment and persuaded her that he was the answer she was looking for. She took the bait and was reeled in before she knew what was happening. It didn't take long for her new boyfriend's true character to reveal itself. He was unstable. He got to know Layla and the things she valued most, then used that information to manipulate and control her. Layla had been living with her mother, her parents having separated on their way to a divorce. Layla's boyfriend convinced Layla and her mother to let him move in. But his erratic behavior eventually drove Layla's mother out of the house. He was verbally, mentally, and physically abusive to Layla, and witnesses did not stop him. He hurled his assaults in front of her mother, her grandmother, and, most regretfully, her two little boys. He could convince Layla that he was redeemable and loving in one moment, then cut her spirit and confidence to the core in the next. And Layla let it happen. Who was she becoming? Before she could come up with an answer, Layla was again pregnant.

Layla had let life happen to her once again. She was staring into a future she did not want and was resigning herself to a life endured, not enjoyed. But this time, it was exponentially worse. She was living with a man who detested her but would not let go. He did not care about her love; he valued her submission. She was his project to mold and control. Everywhere Layla looked, she saw shades of her parents' marriage.

She had been oblivious her whole life, but now she understood. It was like meeting her mother in the role of a wife, for the first time. The conflicts that often arose between Layla's boyfriend and Layla's mother finally made sense. Layla's mom was trying to warn her what to avoid, not mimic, from her own life.

Layla's beautiful baby girl was born, and the clarity became crystal. As Layla held her newborn in the safety of the hospital, she vowed to take back the reigns for her baby's sake. She tried to recollect the moment she first felt like life was passing her by. She should have experienced the joy and hopefulness of college graduation and receiving that diploma. But could she rewind time to make that moment possible? She felt sure that a college degree was the key to the future she could only imagine. She knew she could do it. It would take sacrifice, but she finally had a goal, something she wanted for herself. It was time to stop letting life just happen. With renewed strength and determination, Layla set out to be the mom she wanted to model to her kids.

Once home, Layla's newfound determination waivered. Like many other abused women, Layla began to see her idea of leaving as foolish and impossible. She was penniless, sleep-deprived, and beaten down by a never-ending slew of insults and put-downs. Who was she to think she could make it on her own, let alone pass a college class at 30? Shortly before their daughter's first birthday, Layla finally gathered up the courage to broach the subject of returning to school and was immediately told, "no." When asked why, her boyfriend confided that if Layla went to college, she would get a high-paying job and leave him. She could not understand his reasoning until years later when she realized he feared losing control over her. But Layla's courage was once again gaining ground, and she made a secret visit to the college admissions office. She left the meeting elated at the prospect of returning to school. Her mood changed the second she stepped in the door. Her nice clothes and the scent of the perfume she had worn to the interview were met with suspicion upon her return. Her boyfriend's anger intensified as Layla confessed where she had been and what she wanted to do.

With Layla's mom, grandmother, and sons in the other room, his rage exploded. He threatened to burn down the house with the family inside. He put his fist through their new TV. Then the punches flew at Layla as she protected their daughter in her arms. The strike to Layla's chest landed so hard she feared her lung had collapsed. Hearing the horrific episode in the other room, the family called the police, and an arrest was made. After ten years of abuse, Layla was on her way to freedom.

Layla re-enrolled in college and applied for every grant, scholarship, and loan she came across. She finally had a goal and a true purpose in life, something she wanted for herself. She felt like a new woman, and every right decision was empowering. She took in babysitting to make ends meet. She worked, she studied, she loved on her kids, she brought her mom back into her home. She finished up her associate degree from community college and promptly received a full-ride scholarship to earn her bachelor's degree through the Criminal Justice Department at the university. After graduation, Layla worked as an adjunct professor for her alma mater. She loved the opportunity teaching gave her to build into young adults. Today, Layla picks up the phone to provide encouragement to a single mom, like she does every day. Her diplomas hang on the wall in her office. A framed photo of Layla with her three kids holds a prominent place on her desk. Her business cards rest in a cardholder with her job title: Program Director, Helping Hands for Single Moms.

All of Layla's life experience and education has culminated in this meaningful career role. While working as an adjunct professor and applying to a graduate program, she got a phone call from an old friend and mentor. Helping Hands for Single Moms (HHFSM) was looking for a Program Director. Layla remembered fondly the role HHFSM had played in her life once she plunged into realizing her dream of getting that college diploma.

Among the scholarships that aided Layla through college, the HHFSM scholarship stood apart as a true lifeline. She received dental care for herself and her kids. There were tickets to sporting events and group activities for moms and their families. But most significant, this organization proved to be a source of lasting relationships… a second family of sorts.

The leadership team was made up of real people who were in tune with the unique hurdles facing the single mom student. There was always an ear to listen, a shoulder to cry on, a cheerleader when most needed. They went above and beyond to solve problems. When Layla lost her only means of transportation, they resourced and provided a replacement vehicle. The friends she made through HHFSM were lifelong. So, when Layla was offered an opportunity to sit on the other side of the desk, to be the one reaching out to help a mom in need, she eagerly accepted.

Layla now inspires other single moms to do more than endure life's twists and turns. Her time in the trenches and has equipped her to help others now make that journey. She knows what it is to have an unexpected pregnancy when the timing seems all wrong. She knows the compromises a mom makes to provide some semblance of stability for her child. She understands the incredible self-will it takes to accept the defeats in life and turn against the tide to pursue victory. She remembers hearing and attending to the voice of reason, almost imperceptible, that speaks for your self-esteem and your child's welfare.

Layla has come full circle. She endured, she received comfort, and now she comforts others.

> *"Everything changes when you pursue that degree. Time and time again, I see it happen. It replenishes your confidence. It changes not only the way you see yourself but the way your kids see you. That's a powerful thing.*
>
> *These moms are changing the future for their kids. They are rewriting their children's stories before they even happen. And that's what I share with them. I can see their futures before they can. All they see is homework and deadlines, sacrifice, and hard work. But I know what lies ahead. I know the life they can't yet see. 'Trust the process,' I say.*

'You'll get there.' And they do. I attend the graduations, write the reference letters, and hear the follow-up stories. I see the transformations take place. It's truly incredible.

I'm so grateful for the life I've led… the good, the bad, and the ugly. It's brought me here. And I wouldn't trade any of it for the world. God used it all for good."

Sherie's Story

3

WILL THE KIDS BE OKAY?

Sherie is a Medicare and Medicaid Specialist for a software company in Chicago. She lends her expertise with databases, programming, and problem-solving to serve the nation's healthcare needs.

Sherie raised two daughters: Ruthy and Leah. Ruthy is an IT professional, and Leah is an electrical engineer. Both have found a love for the technology field, following in their mother's footsteps. Sherie and her daughters are accomplished women in the predominantly male career field of technology, but it is the resiliency of Sherie's daughters that makes her the proudest. Their story is one of encouragement for the single moms of young children who fear the unique challenges of single-parent households will forever set back their children's chance to reach their full potential.

Sherie

Single moms work hard, but that taught my kids to work hard. Single moms rely on the kids to pull their weight. That taught my kids commitment to the family community. Single moms must rely on outside help, and that taught my kids to not be afraid to reach out if they have to. When I unexpectedly became a single mom, I worried about what would happen to my girls now that their home was "broken." How would they ever get past all the hurt they were going through?

My goal became suddenly clear…

I would take a less than stellar situation, and together we would learn what to do when things don't go as planned. It was the incentive I needed to be the best mom I could be. I would have to face those hurdles one at a time and deal with them as best as I knew how. We all learned that each struggle is temporary. Whatever the problem, it's not the end of the world. I tried very hard to avoid taking the victim route and instead chose to rise above. That's something I see in my girls today. I'm so very grateful because no matter how I coached them through life's disappointments, the girls ultimately had to choose how to react.

Ruthy

My mom is clever. I am ambitious. I am good at learning new things, and I'm not afraid to try and fail. A lot of that comes from my mom. She taught us that failure is okay. Failure teaches you how not to do whatever you had the courage to attempt. It doesn't mean quit. It just means get back up and do it again, but differently. It's part of the learning process. I think this principle is one of the most valuable lessons my mom taught our family.

Sherie

I was married for 13 years when my husband determined he was gay. With that revelation, he announced that he didn't want to be married to me anymore, and he walked out. Earlier in our marriage, we had left our families behind in Oregon for a career opportunity in Arizona. Three jobs and two cities later, he left me feeling abandoned with my two daughters and no family for support.

I was always a hard worker, but I was not prepared when the bottom fell out. Back in Oregon, after Ruthy was born, I worked as a sign language interpreter for the area schools, but I did not have the money for the four-year degree to become a certified interpreter. When Leah came along, I looked for side jobs that I could do from home since daycare would cost more than I could earn. I took on secretarial work for very small businesses; I did alterations; I made neckties. Once both girls were in school, I took a secretarial position at my church for a nominal salary, no vacation, and no benefits. It was supposed to be supplemental income. Little did I know it would have to support the three of us.

Meanwhile, my husband had started his new life. It was not an amicable separation and communication was often caustic. He was verbally abusive, even in our email correspondence. The court had given him custody on alternating weekends. Honestly, I was fearful every time the girls went to stay with him. I did not know what kind of environment they were walking into.

Ruthy

When we first started staying with my dad in his new world, it was not very "kid-friendly." He was going from boyfriend to boyfriend, and these men would be part of our weekend. Some of it was good, some of it was bad.

Leah

Most of it was bad.

Ruthy

You're right, let's be real. Most of it was bad. There were a few of his boyfriends that were not that nice. I am a part of the LGBTQ community now, and I can tell you that my dad was keeping company with an exceptionally exclusive, self-absorbed crowd. These people had no inter- est in having kids around, and their behavior reflected that.

Leah

We were young kids. It wasn't like Ruthy, and I could leave once we got dropped off for the weekend. We often felt unwanted and unwelcome, even if my dad said he wanted us there.

Sherie

Once my ex was in a stable relationship, things improved, but early on the kids were exposed to a lot of behavior that was hard to explain to them. My girls were 8 and 12 when the divorce happened. The girls, particularly the younger one, were just getting introduced to the basics of sexuality. The environment they visited every other week was not "rated-PG." I had no legal leverage to protect them from what they were exposed to because my husband was not doing anything illegal: no drugs, no assaults. But my girls shared with me the details of their weekends. It drove me crazy and put me in an infinite loop of emotions, so I decided to control what I could. I read a lot and prayed a lot. I had other people pray also, and that gave me power and self-control.

2 Timothy 1:7 tells us that God does not want us to be fearful. We are to respect Him and fear Him like we do the ocean, but we are not to be so afraid that it paralyzes us and keeps us from getting on a boat. While the girls were gone on those weekends, I rested as much as I could so that I would be ready to be all they needed when they came home, and I would have the energy to deal with their 24 hours of anger that always followed their return.

Financially, I knew I had to go back to school if I was going to make it as a single mom. I had always wanted a four-year degree. I knew I was smart, but I needed to prove it to myself. I did a lot of research and looked for careers with a high average starting salary and plenty of job availability. I also considered the typical loans necessary to complete the required degree. I wanted to be sure that my investment of time and resources would be worth it. Originally, I wanted to study graphic design, but the research favored a degree in web development. I didn't have the luxury of following my dreams at this point. I was making a prudent financial decision for my family. I sat the girls down and told them that I was going back to school, that it would take a while to finish, and that it would require all of us working together.

Ruthy

Mom asked us what we would want to do at the end of her program to celebrate. She wanted us to have something we could hold onto when times would get tough so that we would remember there was an end goal we could all enjoy.

Leah

I had just studied WWII in school and gained an interest in war memorials. So, we all agreed on a trip to Hawaii that would include a visit to Pearl Harbor.

Sherie

Hawaii was our goal. So, when my head was buried in books, and it came time for the girls to do the dishes or laundry, I could remind them about the trip, and we all would feel motivated to press on. After graduation, we were able to take that trip. The follow-through was important, and we enjoyed the reward for the sacrifices we made over those years.

Leah

What I remember most about Mom going back to school was the responsibility it added. At eight years old, it was my job to do my own laundry. Later I would plan meals and cook dinner every night for the three of us. Ruthy did the dishes and shopped for groceries from the list I made out. At first, Mom was taking classes at the community college, and that meant an early start for all of us. When she took classes on campus, she would wake us up at 5 a.m. to kiss us goodbye before she left for class. Then we got ourselves up, fed, and out the door for school. She went from class to a full day of work, got home about 13 hours later, then did homework until 11 p.m. But after dinner, we all did homework together, so we felt like we were having family time in the evenings. When she transferred to her online degree program, we didn't have to get up as early, but she still had to fit school in around work.

Ruthy

I don't remember feeling like we were lacking as kids. I always felt like we had what we needed. I knew we were riding the poverty line, but I didn't realize what that meant until my teenage years. Mom was honest about our finances, but it didn't feel like we were going without. We had a roof over our head, food on the table, and my mom was always making sure we had fun along the way. There were incentives to look forward to. Sundays, we went out to a nearby Chinese buffet after church. Once a week, we would rent a movie to watch together. Mom made the little things feel special.

Sherie

When Ruthy got a little older, I gave her a debit card that I funded. That account was specifically for our groceries. The girls had to work together to plan the meals and budget the money. I let them know that if they were able to save anything at the end of the month, we could use that money to go to a movie or eat out. I wanted the girls to be invested in the process of managing household expenses. They didn't ask me for or complain about, things I couldn't provide. They knew what was there. It taught them important life lessons but also gave them successes to celebrate.

Leah

Mom taught us to always look towards a reward. Having an end goal makes the routine and the hard work more meaningful, no matter what it is. That's a life lesson I have taken with me. It has helped me through college, in my career, in life. Those exercises in budgeting and planning have been a great asset to me.

Sherie

I was very open with the girls about every aspect of this new life as the sole provider. When I got divorced, I had to sell the house. I sold it to someone in the church. He allowed us to stay but didn't charge me all that he should have for rent. I was grateful, but when the opportunity to build a Habitat for Humanity house came along, I took it. It was a townhome, one of five units in the building. The program requires 500 hours of sweat equity on the part of the home-owner or immediate fam- ily. Leah was too young, but Ruthy was able to help. They also permitted my mentor to count as a family member since I had none in the state. A certain percentage of the hours can be donated by friends, and I did have people from church come out to help. It took a while to get the hours in. I took two weeks of vacation, and I worked every moment I wasn't sleeping or going to school. I helped with the framing, drywall, insula- tion, clean-up, stocking the store, and updating the logistics for their truck routes. When it was all done, it was so satisfying to actually own a home. It tripled my commute time to live farther out from my place of work, but it was worth it.

Ruthy

We had a very special car that we all loved. It came from Helping Hands for Single Moms (HHFSM). Mom was doing her thing - school, work, construction on the Habitat house - when her old car finally died. Mom brought it to the auto repair shop that did work on cars for the HHFSM scholarship recipients, and they let us know it was beyond repair. At about the same time, a car was donated to HHFSM, and, aware of our transportation dilemma, HHFSM gave it to our fam-ily. It was a lifesaver. Years later, when Mom was finally able to afford a newer car, she let me take over the HHFSM car, and again, it saved us. I used it to run errands and to pick up Leah from school when Mom was working late. It helped me get to my jobs so I could pay for the gas, insurance, and upkeep. I babysat, housesat, cleaned offices at night, and worked in a restaurant. When that car's transmission finally failed beyond repair, we all cried. It had really been a gift to our family in more ways than one.

Leah

I'm really proud of my mom and how she handled everything we went through to get to where we all are today. With all that she was doing to provide for us, it set a really high bar for me when I was getting my degree. If Mom did it with two kids, what was my excuse? It motivated me to make the most of the opportunities to further my education and led to the career that I really enjoy today.

Sherie

I read somewhere that we can only give others what we are used to giving ourselves. I had spent too much of my life accepting guilt. Growing up in a dysfunctional family with lots of drama, I was often unjustly accused, and I learned to accept it. When I got divorced, I took on the blame for not being enough for my husband to hold the marriage together. My self-esteem was non-existent.

But then I began studying God's teaching on forgiveness, and something clicked. I realized that I was forgiven, not because of what I did or didn't do, but because of love and grace. God wanted to do a new thing in my life, but I had to let go of striving for and missing that mark of perfection. I needed to move forward and trust Him, and He would fill in the gaps. I worked on "reparenting" myself. I looked in the mirror and told my reflection the good things about myself I had always wanted to hear spoken to me. I focused on gratitude rather than self-pity. I reminded myself that I had made decisions along the way with the information I had at the time. The hard things were the trials that strengthened my faith. They still do.

This new way of thinking cured me of my false guilt and did wonders for my confidence. And, because I was giving myself the gift of positive thinking, I was better equipped to pass that on to my daughters. While I wouldn't want to go through my life a second time… ever… I also would not trade the lessons I've learned for anything. And my kids learned lessons I might not have thought to teach them. I am so proud and thankful that today they are both independent, capable, bright, and healthy members of society. God was faithful to us.

Michelle's Story

4

WHEN THE END BECOMES
A NEW BEGINNING

*"Although most people thought that a child with special needs
would be the end of me, it really became my beginning."*

S he could not pick him up. All she could do was reach into the
incubator and hold her hand over little David – all 2 pounds, 6
ounces of him. For a moment, this 17-year-old forgot the chaos
of the past 24 hours; the shock of the excruciating waves of pain that
began at the school bus stop; the emergency medical intervention that
failed to stop her premature labor; the Cesarean; the silence in the
room upon delivery; her quiet baby rushed out the door. In her foggy
recollection of the recovery room, she remembers the visit by the lead
pediatrician.

There had been complications. The prognosis was grim. Of course,
the hospital would do everything they could to care for him, however
long that may be. She tried to comprehend it all as she studied the
little life in the glass box, his chest rising and falling amid a tangle of
wires and tubes. How could she fall in love so deeply, so instantly?
How long could he survive? With all of the complications, would he

ever even know how much she loved him? Then, as if answering all of her questions in one reassuring, purposeful motion, David's miniature hand reached out and grasped her finger… and held on.

Life was never easy for Michelle. Her world was tarnished by divorce, neglect, addiction, mental illness, and abuse. Early memories of home life were anything but stable. Her mom worked around the clock to provide for Michelle and her siblings. Her father, living elsewhere, occasionally stopped by the home heavily intoxicated, and little Michelle's job was to help him safely manage the stairs so he could sleep it off. Michelle was first sexually abused at age four. Her mother, haunted by painful memories of her own unresolved abuse, avoided dealing with her daughter's suffering and distanced herself in response.

As life progressed, Michelle began to assume that all the problems surrounding her – her father's alcoholism, her mother's distance and perceived dislike for her, the abuse – were all tied to Michelle's worthiness or lack thereof. She somehow had brought this on herself. Some fatal flaw of hers made her undeserving of a peaceful, happy life.

The chaotic environment that was Michelle's home began to take its toll. She developed anxiety issues and PTSD, although no one took the time to question her odd behaviors. As Michelle spent time around other children her age, even she began to notice that she went about life a bit differently. Instead of walking down the school hallway in line with the rest of the class, something compelled Michelle to plaster her back against the wall and slide cautiously to the next destination. She couldn't sleep unless she was completely covered head to toe by her blanket; she had convinced herself that this was her protective shield should anyone come into her room at night with the intent to do her harm. At 12 years old, Michelle still sucked her thumb.

By middle school, Michelle had enough of letting life happen to her. She sought out ways -consciously and subconsciously - to take back control. She developed an eating disorder and started cutting herself. Learning disabilities (diagnosed later in college) made keeping up in the classroom increasingly difficult, so she lost interest in trying. After years of feeling lost and misunderstood among her family, peers, and teachers, she would no longer be ignored. She was done being the outcast or the invisible kid, she would become the bad girl, and she would give it her all.

Michelle's first serious boyfriend came along during her mid-teenage years. He was the proverbial rebel – violent, reckless, brooding – the attraction was pure adrenaline. Michelle had already settled into life in the fast lane. By her sixteenth birthday, she was engaging in gang activity, drank excessively, used hard drugs, and was physically emaciated by her severe eating disorder. The rebellious pair became an item, and within a few months, Michelle was pregnant.

Michelle's mom, not wanting to raise her troubled teen's baby, told Michelle she could no longer live at home. So when Michelle's boyfriend proposed, Michelle said "yes." Perhaps this pregnancy would be a turning point, Michelle thought. It could be a chance to create the home life she had wanted but never experienced. With this new vision for the future, Michelle got healthy for the baby she was carrying. She believed her husband would do the same, and their fresh new life with their perfect little bundle of joy would begin.

In reality, Michelle found her new home anything but idyllic. In fact, it was worse than the home in which she grew up. The pregnant high school sophomore was now married to an addict who filled her life, not with security and love, but fear and despair. The physical, verbal, and emotional abuse nearly unhinged her. Lost, broken, damaged, hopeless, anxious, and with child, Michelle was deep in a hole, unsure of how she got there, and with no idea how to get out. And then one morning waiting for the school bus, the labor pains began - and Michelle's life changed forever.

The doctors told her to prepare for the worst. David would not make it through the night. He was just too small, too early, and the complications had been too numerous. Yet, here he was, grasping

Michelle's finger as she held her hand over the incubator. He had not moved his limbs since birth. The doctors predicted paralysis. Still, he had he had reached for her. At that moment, she felt what she assumed was the presence of God whispering that David was going to survive.

Michelle had some decisions to make. However long this little life was going to be around, she would need to be courageous. David's birth had defined a purpose for Michelle, and she would have to transform quickly from a rebellious teenager into a capable mother, wife, nurse... all while finishing high school. Less than a year earlier, Michelle was questioning the value of carrying on with life itself. Now, she had a reason for living; a catalyst for change. This pregnancy, this medically fragile baby boy, would quite literally save her life.

The reality of a baby accompanied by the complexities of David's health were terrifying to both parents. For Michelle, she felt incapable of caring for a special-needs child, but what could she do? She already loved him deeply, so she had to try. Her husband, the tough-guy gang member, was just as scared. Still a kid himself, the thought of being the kind of attentive father David would need, overwhelmed him and drove him away. David's birth had shone a spotlight on their volatile, troubled marriage. So, when the law caught up with David's father, and he went to jail, Michelle gathered her resolve and left the relationship once and for all. He was not the father David needed, nor was David the son her husband could accept.

David defied the medical community's expectations. He was surviving. Every day that David's heart beat was a victory. Unfortunately, too many days were tainted by setbacks. After grasping his mom's finger on his very first day of life, he lost mobility in his limbs for the next month and a half. Through the feeding tube, David's little body began to grow, and at the end of four long months in the NICU, Michelle was able to take him home. They were soon wearing a path between home and hospital as David's volatile health continued to present life-threatening emergencies. David's first birthday was a celebration of survival, but his first year concluded with a long list of diagnoses: Hydrocephalus, Epilepsy, Cerebral Palsy, Broncho-Pulmonary Dysplasia, and visual and hearing impairments.

There were things Michelle couldn't control, but there were some things she could. Before David was born, the pregnant teenager resourced an alternative school that would allow her to keep up academically. She made good use of David's first months in the hospital, and by the time she brought him home she was on course to successfully earning her high school diploma. As David grew and the fight for life wore on, Michelle knew she wanted more for her son and herself – but how she would achieve this was unclear. The following years were spent advocating for her son's care through research, phone calls, and countless medical appointments with jargon she did not understand. It wasn't until the 24-year-old Michelle - the mom, the warrior for her son for so many years - had her curiosity piqued and did something for herself. Two close friends were taking college courses to carve out more satisfying career paths. Michelle wondered if she could do the same. A college degree would be a lot of work, but at this point, how much more difficult could it be than what her life had already become?

Michelle gave her mom a call to tell her that she had just enrolled in college. She expected her mom to be proud of the fact that out of the nine siblings in her blended families, Michelle would be the one continuing her education. Instead, her mom's reaction was less than encouraging. She thought Michelle's decision was a foolish distraction, unnecessary, and something that would take her attention and energy away from the task at hand, caring for David. Michelle was devastated, but at the same time, even more determined.

Michelle pressed on once again to defy odds, just like her David. School was a sacrifice, more so than she had anticipated. It was time-consuming. The coursework was difficult after having been away from school for so many years. The challenge was compounded by her dyslexia. Michelle's friends who inspired her to pursue a degree, dropped out. But just as Michelle wondered if she should give up as well, David's nurses became her cheering squad.

Many of them had stories of fighting difficult circumstances to earn their own degrees, and they became essential to Michelle's journey. The first of many divine interventions unfolded when Michelle came across a scholarship program specifically for single moms living at or below the poverty line. Helping Hands for Single Moms (HHFSM), Michelle later recalled, was a "God Whisper."

Michelle had a Judeo-Christian belief in God. She had been to church as a kid. Her stepdad was a good man who had a strong faith. But the older she got and the harder life became, the more she believed that God was indifferent towards her, personally. Then as David came along and Michelle faced some of her most helpless moments, she began to recognize a comforting presence amid the chaos. Could it be the God she had heard about but had never fully experienced, the God of whose love she did not feel worthy? Michelle was desperate to hand over the many, many plates she was trying to keep in motion. Exhausted from doing life in her own strength, Michelle put her faith in Him and surrendered. With God, she knew somehow she would finish this college journey.

Michelle began to see God everywhere at work on her behalf. She called these experiences "God Whispers" – specific reminders that He had not abandoned her but was walking with her through every moment. Life didn't get easier, but God brought calm in the midst of the storm. When David's seizures coincided with midterms or finals, God whispered to Michelle and provided a way to be present both as mother and student. When sleep and hope eluded Michelle in the waiting room during dozens of brain surgeries, God whispered through the hospital nurses in their acts of kindness and timely words of encouragement. And when Michelle needed the help of a village to complete her education, God whispered through a scholarship program that would become a family of support lasting well beyond college.

"Helping Hands for Single Moms has meant the world to us. Not only did it provide me the support I needed to be successful in college, it also equipped me for life. The people I met through the program became the family I needed. There were multiple times that they were used by God to whisper His comfort and guidance to me, and always at just the right moments. When I felt less than capable, overwhelmed, too defeated to see my education through to the end, I would get a random phone call encouraging me and breathing life back into my weary soul! To this day I believe that God sent this program, the staff, and the friends I made for life, as a reminder of His purpose for me!"

Today, Michelle has not one, but two master's degrees. She is the financially independent, sole provider for herself and David, who is now 23 years old. After seven years of teaching special education in the classroom, Michelle decided to run for the local school board. With over 11,000 votes, she won the election. Physically a fully-grown young man, David has lived his life confined to a wheelchair with severe disabilities and brain development that halted at age 3. Together, they have endured David's 34 brain surgeries, countless hour-long seizures, and near-death experiences. With David, Michelle has also experienced world travel, mission trips, surfing, marathons, and inclusion advocacy.

One particular moment for Michelle's journey perfectly captures the incredible woman who stops at nothing to richly love her son. While Michelle was still in the program, basketball tickets were provided to the HHFSM families. Knowing David would prefer sitting with his friends rather than in the special needs seating closer to the court, Michelle lifted her full-grown son from his wheelchair and carried him over her shoulder to the upper reaches of the stadium.

"I never set out to be strong or courageous - nor did I think I ever could be - but David has formed my character. The journey constantly challenges my passions, and although my life became more complicated, our lives together have so much more purpose. David has become my driving force. He saved me from myself. The sacrifices of caring for him never seem that significant when put in perspective. It has been a long, difficult journey. There were multiple times along the way that I was broken physically, mentally, spiritually, financially, and emotionally. There are still nights I pray that God doesn't forget about us. But my life has been filled with His comforting God Whispers reassuring me of His presence. The struggles that once bound us now mark God's glory in our story. I am positive that God hand-selected this precious, fragile little hero to bless me and so many others. His giggles are contagious; his eyes, captivating; his smile; inspiring. My life is proof that God uses the unexpected, the broken, the ones least likely - that is where His glory shines the brightest."

Alicia's Story

5

FINDING STRENGTH THROUGH STEPPING UP

"*You never really understand how strong you are until you have no other choice than to step up. My boys were ages five and four, and the twins were eight months old when I went back to school. I was dealing with diapers, bath time, and potty training, as well as homework, tests, and projects. There were no days off, I had minimal help with the kids and no child support. At times I felt that I had made a mistake taking on school for the hope of a better life and financial position for my family. But I knew that the longer I put things off, the longer it would be until I could change my circumstances. I needed to do this for my kids and myself. When I was in the thick of it, people would ask how I was able to do it all. I just did what I had to do. The position of the absent parent was already taken, so I had to be present.*"

Alicia is a Budget Finance Specialist for the US Marshall's Office by trade, and an active volunteer within the Helping Hands for Single Moms (HHFSM) community. Anyone connected with HHFSM, either as an alum or a current scholarship recipient, knows Alicia's passion to help single moms succeed. She empathizes because she has been there. She never forgot what it was like to find herself suddenly single with four young lives depending solely on her for survival. She remembers the self-doubt, the exhaustion, and the judgment from others. It is a sad reality that when a low-income single mom chooses to improve her earning potential by furthering her education, oftentimes, her decision is questioned or ridiculed by her family and peers rather than encouraged.

Alicia experienced that negativity firsthand. But while Alicia had every reason to accept her fate and surrender to her circumstances, it was not in her nature to do so. Alicia strongly believes in the mission of HHFSM and looks for opportunities to encourage women to transform their futures through education. She has witnessed its impact on the lives of hundreds of women over the years, and she herself is a living testimony to the power of an education.

Alicia was the silent observer as a child. She had an older sister, whose brave and daring personality gave Alicia much to watch and learn, mostly what not to do. Coming from a strict home, Alicia was comfortable staying under the radar and following the rules. Alicia was shy and reserved at school and never had more than one or two friends. She struggled to keep up in school, and in third grade, her teacher diagnosed Alicia with a learning disability.

Her mother was told that Alicia would probably not be able to graduate high school and should be placed in special needs classes. But when the same teacher made Alicia switch her writing hand from left to right, Alicia's mom began to doubt the teacher's credibility and chose to keep Alicia in grade-level classes while working with her at home to keep her daughter on track. By high school, Alicia had successfully implemented the tactics she had learned to compensate for her disability and was not only on schedule to graduate but as an honor student.

Alicia spent so much of her high school years trying to hide her disability and reach her academic goals that she shied away from any sort of social life. Her senior year of high school was made more difficult by the divorce of her parents. Alicia's mom had always been the strong caretaker of the family, but with the dissolution of her 23-year marriage, her mom went into a depression. Alicia's sister had since left home and it

While Alicia was shifting her goals for the sake of others, she did carve out a little time for herself to pursue an interest in modeling. At age 19, Alicia met a woman who owned her own agency, and Alicia signed up as her client. The agent had a son Alicia's age who often hung around the agency. As they got to know one another, the son eventually asked Alicia out on a date. Having little previous experience with romantic relationships, Alicia was a bit naïve when it came to dating. She did not know what standards she should set for herself, what to be wary of, or how to measure a man's words of affirmation against his outward signs of maturity. A year after meeting, the two were married. Alicia was 20, he was 21.

Alicia had proven herself to be responsible when her mother needed her, and she carried that maturity forward into her marriage. Alicia was a diligent employee. She took pride in her work, gained a favorable reputation with her managers, and looked for opportunities to advance. Her husband, on the other hand, had a hard time staying employed. He had always had a woman to take care of him: his mother, his grandmother, and now Alicia. He seemed to be comfortable with that arrangement. Alicia often thought of him as suffering from "Peter Pan Syndrome," never wanting to grow up. He was indecisive and shirked responsibility. He went along with anything Alicia asked because he did not want to have to make decisions and be liable for their outcome. He was in no way desiring to be the head of the household, in fact, at times, Alicia felt he was not that interested in being a partner in the marriage. One tax season he had 13 W2's mailed to him, evidence of 13 different jobs he had accepted then lost. While he struggled to keep a single job, Alicia's instinct kicked in. She rose to the occasion and did what needed to be done, taking on a second job to cover the bills.

A year after marriage, and while working two jobs, Alicia gave birth to her first son. The second son came 15 months later. Alicia kept up with work, and now two children, while her husband still struggled to stay employed. Alicia seriously questioned the health of the marriage. She knew things were off and that her husband did not seem invested in the success of this family, even with two young boys. But Alicia did not like the idea of divorce. There was no real reason to end things, she told herself - no violence, no infidelity - but something was wrong. He was spending time with friends, and sometimes not coming home at all. When he was home, he was distant and disinterested. Alicia confronted him and asked if he wanted to stay married. He, as usual, put the ball in her court. Alicia felt like his inability to answer was, in fact, an answer. She started the divorce proceedings right before she discovered she was again pregnant, this time with twins.

The third pregnancy gave Alicia cold feet. She asked herself, what kind of a mother would leave her children fatherless - four times over – for no *real* reason? She could not bear to give her kids the stigma and the heartache of a broken home. An unmotivated father was better than no father at all, she thought. She decided to do what she could to stay. But five months into the pregnancy, Alicia's husband was coming home less and less. He had apparently joined the softball league at his new job, and it was taking up his evenings. Eventually, Alicia confronted him again about his commitment to their marriage. This time, he responded that he didn't want to be *that guy* that leaves his pregnant wife and two kids. Alicia, reading between the lines, responded, "Well, let's just call it like it is. You are *that guy*." With that, Alicia moved herself and her children into her mother's home.

Alicia's mother still lived in the house where Alicia grew up. There were two extra bedrooms for Alicia and her kids to use. Alicia's mom, recovered from her depression and busy with work, was sorry she did not have more time to help with the kids but was willing to provide space for her grandsons and her pregnant daughter in their time of need. On the day Alicia went into labor, her husband was nowhere to be found. Even his mother could not find him to let him know his children were about to be born.

Three weeks later, Alicia was running some errands when she happened to bump into friends of her husband's. They were the couple that her husband had claimed to be with when he was not at home. Alicia apologized for putting them in the middle of her marital problems and thanked them for letting her husband stay so often. They were confused and said they hadn't seen him for quite a long time. In that moment, the pieces fell into place, and the puzzle was solved. Alicia was not crazy to think that something about her marriage was off. Her husband had been having an affair. This time, when confronted, he owned up to it, and the divorce became final.

The divorce forced Alicia to cast a new vision for her future. She recalled a conversation she had during her pregnancy. Her coworker knew that Alicia was carrying the financial responsibility for her whole family on the insufficient paycheck they both received. She asked Alicia if she wanted to be broke forever. The emotion of this reality check overwhelmed Alicia, and she answered with a tearful "no." Her coworker encouraged Alicia to set a goal, take charge of her life, and get back to school. A few days later, Alicia rehashed the conversation over a visit with her father. Together, they decided she could manage two evening classes per semester for as long as it took to get her degree. Her father offered to split the cost. Now, a couple of semesters under her belt, Alicia had accumulated college credits. As Alicia held her babies and took stock of her predicament, she prayed to God for direction. She sensed she was to go back to school full-time and get a college degree, that this would be the path to providing for her family's future.

Alicia, the one who took care of others, was now in need of support, if only for a few short years. Alicia began by asking her mother if she and the kids could extend their stay to save on rent and her mother graciously agreed. Next, Alicia looked into financial assistance programs and applied for and received the aid she needed to keep her family fed and clothed. Her ex-husband's failure to pay child support only added to her cash assistance and with that came free daycare. Alicia put all the help she received to good use and moved ahead as a full-time student without any student loans or debt. The faster she could get her degree, she told herself, the sooner she could provide for her children entirely on her own.

Alicia's first achievements were two associate degrees, one in Criminal Justice, and the other in Forensic Technology. During her associate degree program, she applied and was accepted as a work-study student and placed in the office of the President of Phoenix College. The office across the hall from the President belonged to the college grant writer. Alicia's ambition caught the attention of the grant writer, and as their friendship blossomed, she received helpful tips on writing effective scholarship applications. Alicia spent countless hours researching and applying for any scholarship, big or small, as she began work on her bachelor's degree. In fact, years later, during a graduation awards ceremony, Alicia had crossed the stage, received her diploma, and took her seat before the listing of all her scholarships was completed. These scholarships made it possible for Alicia to cap off her college journey with a B.S. in Criminal Justice and Criminology, completely debt-free.

One of the scholarships Alicia applied for was awarded by HHFSM. With a GPA of 3.9, she more than met the minimum requirement of a 2.7 GPA. She conducted an in-person interview and received an acceptance call a few weeks later. The HHFSM scholarship program immediately set itself apart from the others Alicia had received. The staff wanted to get to know her. They checked in just to see how she was holding up. They asked questions like, "how can we make this better for you?" The program gathered their recipients together at meetings to connect, share, and network. The once shy and introverted Alicia formed real, lasting friendships. She found women who understood in one way or another what she was going through because they had similar experiences. No longer did Alicia feel isolated and alone. She had found her people, a place to give, and a place to receive.

In her final semester, Alicia received an internship with the US Marshals Office near home. Three days before graduation, she was granted a position as a contract worker, and in the years since she has successfully climbed the ranks to her current position in the Finance department. Alicia is grateful for life's new chapter. She owns a new car, a house, and earns double the salary of the job she quit to go back to school.

Her family is well cared for, her financial responsibilities are covered, she loves her career, and she even got remarried.

> *"I received a lot of criticism for going back to school when I did. People didn't understand how I could take on college while the kids were so young. Because of the pushback, I worried that my kids would be traumatized or upset with me. The reality is that they didn't even notice. They never saw the struggle; they never felt the sacrifice. We were together, I loved on them, and that's all they wanted.*
>
> *Life is a learning experience. There are choices you make along the way that you can't take back. You have to accept the mistakes and then move forward to make them better. That's how you gain wisdom. I have a quote from Henry Ford that has become a motto for me, 'Failure is simply the opportunity to begin again, this time more intelligently.' I want single moms to know that their story is not yet written. If you don't like your circumstances, change them. If you're working on change, keep going. And find good people to encourage you on your journey."*

Michelle's Story

6

LEAVING A LEGACY
FOR YOUR CHILDREN

"One of life's greatest sources of joy is being called somebody's parent. But that blessing comes with responsibility. We, as parents are to provide as much stability and nurturing as possible, even though our children may not seem to realize or appreciate the sacrifices we are making. They don't always see what's happening behind the scenes. We might be working through the painful circumstances that led to becoming a single parent. We might be dealing with an ex-spouse who is a negative influence on our children. Regardless of the emotions, our specific circumstances may be causing, we are called to place our children's needs above our own. Be assured, the Lord receives our selfless caring as acts of worship to Him because they reflect the spirit of Christ who, 'made himself nothing, taking the very nature of a servant." (Philippians 2:7)

Michelle shares these words of encouragement from the perspective of both mother and child. Michelle, the single mom, knows the heartache of letting go of a codependent relationship for the sake of becoming the healthy role model her daughter deserves. Michelle, the corporate professional, owes her success to her own single mom who modeled perseverance through any and all adversity. To unfold Michelle's story, it must begin with the remarkable woman who raised her.

Michelle's mom, Patrice, never shied away from challenges. In fact, one could say she went looking for them. Patrice came from a solid family of high achievers. Patrice had a brother who worked for NASA as an aeronautical engineer. Not to be outdone, Patrice served in the U.S. Military in the late 1970s through the early 1980s when the country was still grappling with the concept of a woman in uniform. But like many soldiers, once she became a civilian, she struggled to find her place in society.

Patrice gave birth to two daughters. She made a home for her family amidst the public housing projects of New York in the borough of Yonkers. The surrounding neighborhood was a hotbed of crime and violence, poverty, and hopelessness. But inside the four walls of Patrice's apartment, she created an oasis - warm, stable, and safe. Patrice embraced motherhood and worked hard to cover both parental roles. The girls' dad was long gone before Michelle had any recollection, and Patrice never spoke ill of him. With love and determination, Patrice was confident that she could raise Michelle and her sister simply fine on her own. There was only one thing that threatened to get in her way. She was an addict.

Patrice would not let addiction define her. It was something she did, not who she was. But as time went on, she knew the drugs were getting in the way of her goals, so she began to pursue recovery. The grip of drug use was stronger than she realized and the road to freedom was longer than she had anticipated. In the end, it took nine stints in rehab to gain sobriety. Michelle recalls tagging along to Narcotics Anonymous meetings, doing homework in the back of the room while listening to the devastation drugs had caused... lost families, HIV, prostitution. Michelle knew this was reality. She saw it in the neighborhood, but her own experience of life with an addict was different. Patrice refused to lean into the stereotype of the addict in the projects. She wanted more for her girls and for herself and knew this was just another challenge to overcome.

Patrice's struggles may have landed her in subsidized housing, but she took her community on as a mission. Everywhere she looked, she saw opportunities to affect change in what was often a dark and dangerous place. She became heavily involved with a literacy program in the community. She had a gift for inspiring others towards self-improvement and challenged those around her to reach their full potential. Michelle recalls a particular afternoon when the girls and Patrice were heading out of their building via the stairwell because the elevator was in disrepair, as usual. As they descended, a well-known drug dealer slowly approached them. Protecting her girls, Patrice pinned them against the wall then turned to face the drug dealer. She asked him what he needed. The drug dealer took Patrice into his confidence and explained that he wanted her help. He couldn't read. Patrice began to tutor him in her living room. Soon, others started coming for help, and a makeshift reading program took form in her apartment. The tenant association learned about Patrice's initiative and offered both funding and space to make her program official.

Patrice lived her faith out loud. She did not keep her relationship with God in a box saved for Sundays, and her girls watched and learned. She openly brought her struggles to the Lord, asking for strength, change, and release from addiction. Michelle and her sister witnessed Patrice's faith and learned from it. They realized even from a young age that God was real, He could handle anything, and He really did answer prayer.

God was bringing new opportunities to Patrice. It was the early 1990's, and she was two years sober when she was chosen to participate in a new public housing initiative. Qualified candidates from urban homes were moved into suburban subsidized housing where it was theorized that these families might thrive. What the housing authority could not anticipate were the reactions of those suburban residents not in favor of the program. Patrice and the girls were placed in a predominantly white, affluent neighborhood. A public bus ran a limited route with no other passengers but their family of three. Without a car, the girls rode their bikes or walked with Patrice to complete the routes the bus did not run.

Additionally, the targeted racial slurs, vandalism, and false accusations took away from seemingly better opportunities. In spite of the pushback, Patrice tried her best to make a home for her girls. Even on their long walks and bike rides, Patrice and the girls could be heard singing their favorite gospel songs in three-part harmony.

Patrice was working four jobs: retail sales, newspaper delivery, security, and the corner deli counter. The pace to make ends meet was exhausting. Unbeknownst to the girls, Patrice had been in contact with Michelle's father. He offered to help out if they were willing to move to Arizona. The cost of living was lower, and his extended family were eager to help with the girls. It was an attractive offer, and the timing was ideal, so they loaded up a rental truck and made the trip out west.

Settled in her new home, Michelle gravitated towards the church. She enjoyed the teaching, the programs, and the people. If the doors were open, she was there. While being the new kid at school made it difficult to form friendships, the church always had a place for her. As she grew into a teenager, Michelle's spiritual maturity caught the attention of church leadership. She was comfortable and articulate in group settings. She encouraged others with words of wisdom and affirmation. By high school, Michelle was invited to participate in a public speaking ministry and began delivering motivating messages to teens on the local church circuit.

School was a different story. Michelle had difficulty finding social acceptance among her new classmates. Feeling like an outsider, she eventually lost her motivation to attend classes. Her school absences added up such that by the end of her junior year of high school, she was informed that she would not have enough credits to graduate on schedule. Michelle's academic counselor suggested she transfer to an alternative high school program where she could make up for the lost time. Once enrolled, she had to add an additional online class and a night class to meet her graduation requirements. That final school year, Michelle spent 15 hours a day, five days a week on campus. She would arrive at 6:00 am to meet a teacher who let her into the building so she could use the school's internet. Her regular class day ran from 8 am to 2 pm. She completed homework until the start of her night class that ran from 4:30 to 8:30. Her academic advisor did not think that Michelle would be able to keep up with the workload, but by the end of the second semester, Michelle received her diploma.

Patrice's little girls were becoming adults. It had been a long journey, but she felt that she had given her daughters the foundation and life lessons they would need to succeed. Now it was time for her to think about her own future. Patrice reenlisted with the National Guard and, shortly after, was stationed in Iraq.

As Patrice headed to the Middle East, Michelle was a high school graduate living on her own, working in a Christian bookstore, and hanging out with her friends. The alternative school had introduced Michelle to a peer group different than her church friends. They were an edgier crowd with different morals and behaviors, but they were very accepting of Michelle, something she did not feel among her classmates in the public high school. Michelle began to let their influence impact her, and she started making moral compromises. She was conflicted because she still had a vibrant church life. As a speaker and youth leader, she knew that she could not last long leading two opposing lives. The hypocrisy weighed heavily on her heart. But when a friendship with a young man from her new circle turned intimate, she stepped down from ministry, left the church, and avoided God.

As Michelle pursued this romantic relationship, she began to change. It was a gradual drift from the young woman she once was as she gave up little pieces of her character bit by bit. Four years into the relationship, a compromised Michelle caught her boyfriend cheating. Still wanting to keep a relationship that was clearly not meant to be, Michelle decided to forgive him, and soon after became pregnant. Then, partway into the pregnancy, the police caught up with her boyfriend for criminal activity. He was indicted and sentenced to three years in jail, and Michelle was left to carry on with her pregnancy alone.

Michelle took a look at her life and couldn't believe where she had landed. But taking a page from her mother's book, she would not let the consequences of her decisions defeat her. There was redemption to be found in this difficult circumstance. Unable to afford her apartment on her own, Michelle began problem-solving. By divine providence, she found a local shelter for pregnant women that just happened to have availability. Michelle moved in, received the prenatal care she was lacking, and three months later, she brought her precious daughter into the world.

The shelter became home for nearly a year. It was beautiful and comforting, an ideal place for the emotional healing that would occur. The other women at the shelter had lived hard lives marred by physical abuse, addiction, and homelessness. As stories were shared, Michelle reflected on her own life story and realized God's hand of protection throughout. She was homeless, her baby's father was in jail, but she had been spared far worse. Her soul was finding its voice once more.

Michelle flourished in the shelter. Being her bubbly and optimistic self, she made quick friends with the staff and volunteers. She found more in common with this group of women than her fellow residents. These women were inspiring to Michelle, and she felt she could aspire to be one of them. They were leading lives of purpose and bringing value to others. They were filled with wisdom and encouragement. They were educated. The seed was planted, the vision cast, and soon after leaving the shelter, Michelle took her first step to change the course of her destiny. She enrolled in community college. Throughout the next few years, Michelle found herself in a good place mentally, physically, emotionally, and spiritually. She had her little girl, a place to live, a job, and a plan for the future. But life was about to throw another challenge her way.

Three and a half years after his incarceration, Michelle's boyfriend was released and in need of a place to stay. She knew it was a risk to take him in, but the idea of having a real family outweighed her misgivings. After all, she thought to herself, she was stronger now and he wanted to get to know his daughter. What could be the harm? Michelle was convinced that this time, she could be with her boyfriend without losing herself. But no sooner had he moved in than the drama began. Michelle had changed, but he had not. That gravitational pull he had on her was still there. Once again, it was a battle between two ways of life, and as much as she wanted it to be different, Michelle knew her way would never win out. Why couldn't she just break things off? Then one day, she made the connection. He was her addiction. He was unhealthy for her, but she was afraid she could not live without him.

Now that she saw it, she knew what to do. She prayed to God for strength, for change, and for release from this addiction, just like her mom had done so many years ago. Again, God answered… in a most unexpected way. The police came looking for Michelle's boyfriend, this time for a parole violation. He was incarcerated once more, and Michelle was released.

Trying to mitigate some of the unravelings of her own wellbeing from the drama with her boyfriend, Michelle went back to church. Immediately, she felt at home. She surrounded herself with uplifting people that shared her faith and held her accountable. She met spiritually mature women who came alongside her and helped her to overcome her codependency on, and addiction to her boyfriend, to realize her self-worth, and to get her thinking back on solid ground. For the first time, Michelle felt like she was really adding knowledge to her faith and acting on principles, not just feelings. It was empowering. She forgave her boyfriend for their past, took responsibility for her role in the drama, and was finally able to mentally leave the relationship for good.

It was a long road, but Michelle pursued her college degree. At times she had to lighten her class load to keep her little family going, but she pressed on, adding classes as she could. She researched and applied for scholarships to fund her ambition. She was rewarded not only with tuition resources but meaningful mentors who cheered her on. Some of these relationships outlasted her college journey, including the friends she made through Helping Hands for Single Moms (HHFSM). There were many times Michelle felt like giving up on her goal, but her new friends at HHFSM encouraged her to just keep pushing through her fears of failure until the belief in herself came back. And it did.

College graduation day finally arrived. Michelle's mom, who had retired from the military to Florida, came into town to watch her daughter graduate Cum Laude. As Michelle was getting ready to leave her apartment for the big day, she spied Patrice standing before a mirror trying on Michelle's cap and gown. It touched Michelle's heart to see her mom envisioning herself in Michelle's shoes.

Michelle also had a moment of her own. She remembered the oasis of comfort her mom had created in the urban housing project. She recalled Patrice's positive spin on every hardship. She thought about the inspiration her mom had brought to people even when Patrice could have used some encouragement herself. Michelle had never seen this woman feel sorry for herself, make excuses, or raise the white flag of surrender. Patrice did more than face challenges that came her way, she ran at them. Today's diploma would be for Michelle – for all the hard work, the sacrifices, the fight for self-respect, and the determination to live her best life. But it would also be for Patrice... for the same reasons. Patrice would be the mom of a college graduate. Both women would receive validation that no one could ever take away, a symbol of achievement, proof of a mission accomplished.

Jacinda's Story

7

EVERY DAY IS A DO-OVER!

"I just wanted to sleep. I wanted to pretend that this wasn't happening. I had been out cold for three straight days, but I felt like I could sleep forever."

"Hon, you have to wake up now."

"Who was this woman, and what did she want from me?" Jacinda struggled to sort reality from her prolonged dream state.

"You brought your son with you. You need to wake up. We had people babysitting your child, but you have to get up now and take care of him. He needs his mom."

It was all coming back – her toddler, the baby in her womb, the violent father of her unborn child, the drugs, the rehab facility she had checked herself into… this was Jacinda's literal wake-up call.

Jacinda had always been fiercely self-reliant. She was in third grade when her parents divorced. Now the sole provider, Jacinda's mother worked both day and night shifts as a waitress, and in the hours that remained, she cleaned houses. Her mother's tireless work schedule left Jacinda home alone too often. Regularly unsupervised, she became known among neighboring parents as sort of a wild child. She didn't have any obligations after school, she didn't have to be home in time for dinner, she didn't have a curfew. Some families saw what was going on and tried to help out by bringing Jacinda along with their own kids to camps, scouts, or sports. Jacinda was happy to have the friendships and something to fill up her free time.

One of the local churches sent a bus around the neighborhood to transport kids to youth groups and Vacation Bible School. Prompted by friends, Jacinda decided to give religion a try. Most of the other kids had traditional families, homes headed by two parents and filled with siblings, and minivans that waited in the carpool line for pick-up after church activities. As Jacinda walked past the other kids to board the bus alone that would take her to an empty house, the experience left her feeling isolated and somewhat jealous. She eventually stopped going.

Jacinda missed her dad terribly. In her mind, it was easy to choose sides after the divorce. The way she saw it, her mother had selfishly broken up the home by leaving her father. Her dad's only fault (as far as she could comprehend in her limited understanding) was that he liked to drink. In reality, Jacinda's dad was having a difficult time being responsible for himself, let alone a wife and child. He struggled with alcohol addiction and spent most of his time and resources in bars. After the divorce, he moved into a dilapidated trailer with a damaged roof that barely provided shelter from the elements. Jacinda saw it all through rose-colored glasses. She loved every moment of being with her dad, even if she did spend most of her visits in a battered booth at the local bar.

As the years went by, Jacinda continued to piece together her own theories and assumptions regarding her parents and, in the process, constructed a strong resentment against her mother. No longer was Jacinda going to play the role of the little girl who tried to keep under the radar while her mom worked long hours to provide. As she grew up, Jacinda turned a corner and became increasingly expressive and vindictive.

She destroyed things in the home to spite her mom. She lashed out in anger and ridicule. And when her mom left for the occasional date,

Jacinda spewed horrible, hurtful names at her. Jacinda had become the stronger personality of the two and used her emotional outbursts to control the home. What she could not control was her mother's relationships. In Jacinda's eighth grade year, her mom got serious with a man who would later become her stepdad. He was a cop. He took one look at the dynamics of this dysfunctional home life and advocated for change. Jacinda would have none of it. She ran.

Jacinda was already socializing with a delinquent crowd at school. She was using drugs and making poor decisions with the rest of her crowd. When she made the decision to run away, she didn't have to go far to find a willing accomplice. Her boyfriend at the time invited her to tag along with his transient family who were moving a few cities away. Her boyfriend's family was less than wholesome. They supported her drug use and had no concerns about harboring a 13-year-old runaway. But Jacinda was back to living her life unsupervised and on her own terms, so she stuffed any feelings of regret and settled in.

Back home, Thanksgiving came and went. Christmas passed without a word from Jacinda. Day after day, Jacinda's mother willed herself to carry on with no information regarding the whereabouts of her daughter. Then one day, Jacinda got sick. She had a severe case of strep throat and needed medical attention. Miserable and far from home, Jacinda longed for the comfort of her mom, so she decided to return. Her mom was relieved that she was back, but one look at her emaciated, drug-addicted daughter, and she knew Jacinda needed help beyond what a mother could provide. Making what she believed to be a wise decision, Jacinda's mom admitted her daughter to a behavioral health facility… strep throat and all. This was not what Jacinda was envisioning upon her return, and her resentment against her mother reached new heights. Jacinda was released to her mother's care a month later, brought back home, and in another act of defiance against authority, Jacinda ran away before the next sunrise.

Over the following year, Jacinda waffled between what was expected and what she wanted. She tried coming home again, only to serve another unsuccessful stint in the behavioral health facility against her will. Jacinda's issues continued to mount, and her mother knew her daughter needed professional help. Jacinda stayed in high school long enough to earn 3 credits. At that point, she knew she had to make a choice between maintaining her schooling or her drug addiction. The addiction won. So, as her peers were attending homecoming dances, joining sports or clubs, and getting a driver's license, Jacinda was in another world.

Her social influences migrated from teenage experimentation to a detrimental culture of violence and criminal behavior. What began as Jacinda's attempt to punish her mom for daring to marry another man, evolved quickly into a lifestyle she could no longer control. The grip was so strong it would be many years before she could escape.

Her first pregnancy resulted in a son. Soon after the birth, his father went to prison. Jacinda was now an addict as well as a single mom. Her family wanted to help by caring for the baby, giving him a healthy home with safety and stability, while Jacinda took as long as she needed to get sober in a rehab facility. But unlike many addicts, Jacinda bonded with her son and could not even consider separation. He was her lifeline. His existence motivated her to care for more than herself... to try and break her destructive habit.

Still, Jacinda could not shake her addiction.

In October 2005, Jacinda was four months pregnant with her second child from a different father, who was also an addict. One evening, as an argument escalated, he pulled a gun on Jacinda. As she tried to drive away, he shot at the moving vehicle. The tires were blown out and the car was sprayed with bullets. Terrified, Jacinda ran for it. In an attempt to hide herself, she dove into the brush along the road. Her heart was beating uncontrollably, and her mind raced. She imagined her son losing his mom. She pictured her unborn child dying in the womb.

The consequences of her decisions were now putting those she loved most at the greatest risk. Time passed, and by some miracle, her boyfriend, gun in hand, never found her. From her cell phone, she reached out to her mom and stepdad. They picked her up and brought her and her two-year-old son to their home and listened as she talked about the need for a change. Not wasting any time, Jacinda looked up information on recovery programs that would take a pregnant woman and her child, and the very next day she self-admitted to a "mommy and me" rehab facility. She slept for three days straight.

The years submerged in a culture riddled with crime, violence, and people out of their minds on drugs were a walk in the park compared to the fear Jacinda felt entering rehab. Here, she had to leave behind her entire world – her home, her friends, and her freedom to deal with her drug habit on her own terms. She wanted to leave. Like a caged lion, she would pace along the gates contemplating escape. She'd think to herself, "I have to get out of here. I have to get high. Today I'm going to make a run for it." But she never did. Day by day, moment by moment, God gave her the strength to stay just a little longer. She knew it was God at work, and He did not fail her. Slowly, she began to heal.

Jacinda spent the better part of a year in the recovery facility. She delivered a healthy baby girl. She was taught how to be a mom to both of her children. She learned how to live sober. Over time, Jacinda and the kids moved to a transitional living facility for victims of domestic violence. She feared the instability of her daughter's father and had heard through the grapevine that he was still on the streets. From the safety of the facility, she spent a year and a half gaining life skills and laying the groundwork for her next chapter of life.

Now sober, Jacinda began to assess her potential. With fresh eyes, she observed some of the other women she met through recovery. They had families that loved them. They were well-dressed and took care of their appearance. The cups they brought to meetings showed that they could afford specialty coffees from trendy shops. Sure, they were also dealing with addiction, but aside from that, their lives looked much prettier than the world Jacinda had known. She needed a fresh vision for her own future. She didn't want to go anywhere near the chaos and struggle that marked her old existence. She wanted healthy relationships. She wanted financial stability for her family. SHE wanted to sip fancy coffees. Part of her recovery was setting and reviewing goals on a daily basis. Armed with a new purpose, she needed a key goal that would make the rest attainable. She wanted a college degree.

Positive affirmation was a new concept to Jacinda. As She was now making better choices for herself and her kids, and others were noticing and showing their support. Her caseworkers recognized her potential right away. Typically, years of drug use took a terrible toll on addicts, both physically and mentally. Once Jacinda got sober, however, she was fresh, healthy, and mentally sharp. Caseworkers encouraged her to press on with her goals, asserting that with the intelligence and ambition she possessed, the only limitations would be those of her own invention. She had what it would take to succeed.

One of Jacinda's greatest inspirations for going back to school, ironically, was her mom. While Jacinda was still disconnected and out in the world, her mom went to college and earned a degree. In fact, her mom graduated the same year Jacinda entered rehab. In recovery, Jacinda learned to let go of the built-up resentment against her mom, take ownership for her own faults in the tumultuous relationship, and understand and appreciate the woman she once unjustly blamed.

The two sought forgiveness from one another and began anew. The humbled Jacinda wanted a new identity to go along with her fresh start, something other than the "recovering drug addict" label that would always be a part of who she was. Despite missing so much school during the dark days of her teen years, Jacinda had managed to earn her GED. So, when Jacinda looked with admiration upon her mother – the strong single mom who never gave up on her daughter, labored tirelessly to provide for her family, and recently earned a college degree – she saw the role model that would guide her to the woman she wanted to be.

Early in her program, one of Jacinda's professors recognized her potential and admired her noble pursuit of an education as a means to create a better life for herself and her children. The professor also understood the particular challenges that single moms face earning a degree while taking full care of two small kids. With a heart to help and a desire to see Jacinda succeed, he pointed Jacinda towards a scholarship program designed to help women just like her. Grateful, Jacinda applied and was soon awarded a scholarship from Helping Hands for Single Moms (HHFSM). Little did she know the lasting impact this program would have on her college years and beyond.

Despite the support of those around her, Jacinda still had to do the hard work herself. She had not been in a traditional classroom, sober, since 7th grade. As she tackled her general education requirements for her degree program, math became her greatest obstacle and threatened to block her newfound goal. HHFSM kept in regular contact with Jacinda, offering a listening ear in addition to tangible help. During those academic struggles, Jacinda would call Joanne, her new friend, and program director, often in tears and ready to give up. Jacinda felt that perhaps she had aged out of the college opportunity window. Joanne listened with great empathy. She put Jacinda in contact with tutors who walked her through her toughest subjects, and more than once would remind Jacinda, "It's okay to want to quit – just don't."

The HHFSM community became essential companions on Jacinda's college journey. The money was, of course, much needed and appreciated. The dental care was a privilege never before afforded to Jacinda or her kids. She welcomed free auto service so she could safely transport her family to and from wherever they needed to be. But the most remarkable aspect of the program was the opportunity to witness Godly men and women live out their faith. Jacinda was particularly impacted by the founder, Chris Coffman. Like many of her fellow HHFSM scholarship recipients, she had never known a Christian role model, especially a man. Chris prayed with the moms specifically and regularly. He listened. He cared. He didn't just talk about supporting Jacinda and her fellow scholarship recipients, he took action. He followed up. And he did it all without any hidden agendas or selfish motives. As a mom raising a son, this gave Jacinda hope. As a believer in the God of the Bible, Jacinda was inspired by Chris, Joanne, and all the faithful people she met through the program to now boldly live out her own faith.

College was transformative not just for Jacinda, but her son and daughter as well. HHFSM organized regular family events for moms and their kids to connect with one another and create memories together. There were NBA games, zoo visits, ice cream fests… all kinds of activities. The kids began to associate mom's college education with fun. As the kids grew, they would do homework with mom, feeling the comradery of sharing in the academic experience. Jacinda continued to remind them that good things happen when you are doing good things for yourself.

Eleven years after entering rehab, Jacinda graduated with a B.A. in Public Administration while maintaining a 4.0 GPA. She currently works as a Health Inspector for the county and loves her career. She owns her own home. Her teenagers are college-bound. Jacinda's mom and stepdad are an integral part of her family's lives. She talks to her mom three times a day. They couldn't be closer. The "cop" stepdad that Jacinda fought so hard to push out of the family has been an amazing father figure to them all. He has been the babysitter, school volunteer, and "sports grandpa" cheering the kids on. He has been a greater blessing than Jacinda could have ever imagined.

"I didn't expect to live. I was making choices in my life just assuming that I would eventually die as a drug addict, but in the meantime, I would have fun. Never in a million years did I picture myself with a bachelor's degree, a home, and really good kids!

The irony of my job now is that I wear a badge. I spent so much of my life being afraid of anyone with a badge. I'm proud now to wear one myself. To me, it is representative of my journey, and the second chance I was given at life. I left my former ways behind, accepted God's forgiveness, and began to love myself. Something I learned along the way is that if you don't like the choices you made yesterday, you don't have to make the same ones today. I love that idea. We get a do-over every day our eyes open. I am so grateful that God awakened me to a fresh start."

Sy's Story

8

KEEP PUSHING FORWARD

"*My advice to single moms would be to NEVER do NOTHING. In other words, keep pushing forward. Sometimes all you can do is take baby steps... chip away at your goals and your challenges little by little. But you can take down those mountains one pebble at a time. You can't let your past become your excuse for not having a future. Your kids are your motivation for change. Life comes at us, and we don't just have ourselves to worry about, we're responsible for their well-being. It can be scary, draining, demanding, and lonely as a single mom. But life is going to keep moving, your kids are still going to be there needing you, and every day is another opportunity to make the best of it. So just keep putting the work in, until it works out.*"

The journey to Sy's four-year college degree was riddled with obstacles, but she was determined to get her diploma. Focused and unshakeable, she hurdled each challenge that came her way. But in the home stretch with just a few months left to go before graduation, Sy was ambushed with one devastating blow after another that threatened to undo her, or at least throw her off course for a while. A disheartening breakup, a fatal accident, a ruinous fire... for Sy, they hit one after the next. Any single one of these grave circumstances would have been enough to derail most anyone. With each tragedy, she had a choice to make, should she accept defeat, or could she possibly muster the strength to fight another day?

Sy likely inherited her grit from her military parents. When the couple met in southern California, Sy's mother was an accountant in the Marines, and her father was a field nurse in the Navy. Both made a great impact through their service. Sy's mother was a trailblazer as a female Marine at a time when it was still an anomaly for a woman to make the cut. Sy's dad worked in obstetrics and helped with labor and delivery for military families. Both mother and father brought sons to the marriage, the two oldest from mom and the youngest from dad. Sy was the child that unified her parents. Soon after Sy was born, the blended family opted for change, left their military lives, and moved to Ohio.

It was difficult being the baby sister with three very busy older brothers. The boys' activities with school and sports crowded Sy's childhood, and she often felt neglected. Her parents were also distracted by their marital issues. Unable to resolve their differences, the marriage did not last longer than a few years. And most damaging and unbeknownst to anyone, Sy was being molested by a member of the extended family. Confused and ashamed, she compartmentalized her secret trauma and carried on as if nothing was wrong.

After the divorce, Sy's mother had to quickly carve out a sustainable life for her two boys and little girl. She found subsidized housing on Cleveland's east side and found work managing a grocery store bakery and clerking at the local Kmart. Two jobs meant long hours away from home and extra responsibilities shouldered by the kids, but everyone did their part. Thankfully, no one in Sy's family realized the drama that was unfolding in the neighborhood. While Sy's mother was doing her best to provide a safe home for her children… nearby, a soon-to-be notorious criminal was preying on women, abusing and often murdering his victims. Anthony Sowell, the Cleveland Strangler, was finally caught in 2009 and convicted as a rapist and serial killer. The

FBI discovered the corpses of 11 of his victims, some of them, local residents, buried in and around his home just a few doors away from Sy and her family.

Sy's father moved in with Sy's grandmother in a better part of town. He made a home for himself, his son, and his shared custody of Sy. Knowing the conditions plaguing the public schools of east Cleveland, he enrolled his daughter in a private school of the arts for her elementary education. Sy had a knack for drama, and her parents agreed that the private school would give her an academic head start. While Sy didn't care much for school, she did love spending time with her dad.

Her mother was an efficient household manager but lacked emotional warmth, so Sy did not feel that special mother-daughter bond as a child. Sy's father, however, was lovingly demonstrative and made it known that Sy was the apple of his eye. Sy spent every free moment by her father's side, whether working on the car or cooking dinner. Ever the soldier, Sy's father provided the kids with structure, setting boundaries, and giving out chores. But once the responsibilities were taken care of, they were free to have fun. Sy appreciated her father's parenting style and, as children do, imagined growing up to be like him. For Sy, that meant becoming a nurse. Sy would first have to navigate her way through school. By now, Sy was exhibiting signs of suppressed sexual abuse that no one, including herself, could diagnose. She instinctively dissociated when she became stressed or anxious, but her parents and teachers saw it as a self-controllable "attention" issue to be overcome, rather than a coping mechanism she had unknowingly adapted. Socially, she was shy and withdrawn. She lacked self-esteem and feared that getting close to friends might lead to the discovery of her secret shame, so she kept to herself. She had little control over her emotions. She often felt sad, anxious, angry, or apathetic and her feelings were palpable. By 6th grade, Sy was beyond what the private school could handle, labeled a "troubled youth" by school counselors, and sent to public school with her mom's sons in east Cleveland.

The transition was initially positive. Sy had nearly perfect attendance for the first two years. Her closest brother was charged with walking Sy to school every morning, and because Sy respected her brother, she got in line. Small victories and a fresh start did much to build her self-confidence and positive outlook throughout middle school. But then the boys moved on to college, Sy's mom was busy with work, and Sy was left alone to manage her thoughts and fears. Once again Sy lost her way, she retreated to her old coping mechanisms, and her academics and behavior suffered. Sy was letting her past trauma defeat her. She needed a new, more empowering view of self, and high school athletics provided that opportunity. By junior year she made the track team. She found untapped strengths within herself and made friends in the process. The competitive atmosphere was good for Sy. Her new peer group was made up of the school's high achievers - honor students and college-bound. Not wanting to be left behind, Sy doubled down on her efforts at school and pulled up her GPA. She was smart. The previous year she had aced the Ohio Graduation Test, a cumulative knowledge exam given to students in 10th grade.

But by senior year, she realized her efforts were too little too late. While her friends were getting early acceptance letters from colleges across the country, Sy had to deal with the damage she had done to her academic record the previous years. Still, her grades and test scores were enough to get her accepted to a nursing program at a small Catholic college in southern Ohio. With little oversight from anyone, she filled out the complicated FASFA documents, signed the acceptance letter and financial agreement, and off she went.

Campus life suited Sy. She was conquering her demons, focusing on her future, and fitting in with the college crowd. When she was called to the financial aid office near the end of her freshman year, she had no idea that she was about to hit a serious setback. Sy was informed that her identity had been stolen years earlier and now her Financial Aid for college tuition was in jeopardy. In addition, her FASFA documents had been filed incorrectly and as a result, she could not take out any more tuition loans and she had missed the opportunity for grants for which she should have qualified, had her paperwork been in order. She would have to forgo college until her financial issues could be sorted out. Sy had no other choice but to return home.

Sy's mom had moved back to California almost immediately after dropping Sy off at her dorm the previous fall, so Sy moved in with her dad. She felt like a failure having to drop out of college. All hope, however, was not lost. Sy knew now that her dream of becoming a nurse was possible. It would take hard work and a different route, but she was not willing to give up. Sy immediately got a full-time job at Walmart and began working to repair her credit and pay off debt.

But in the interim, Sy got sidetracked. She began spending time with a man she had met at work, much to her father's dismay. One thing led to another, and soon Sy discovered she was pregnant. Her father hated to see his daughter in this situation but felt the last thing she needed was coddling. He told Sy she had to go back to college or move out on her own, but that either way, she had to step up and take charge of her future. Sy left her dad's house upset by the ultimatum and slept in her car for a while until she found an apartment.

She thought about the two choices her father had given her and decided to prove something to him and to herself... she kept her full-time job to support herself, AND she went back to school. She had just enough time to become a Certified Nursing Assistant (CNA) before her delivery date. It wasn't her end goal, but it was a step in the right direction, and it would get her a job in the healthcare field. The pregnancy became the motivation Sy needed to get back on track.

Sy knew she had no future with the father of her baby girl. For one thing, he was already married. In fact, the day Sy found out about the pregnancy she sent a text to the father, and that text was intercepted by his wife. The wife was rightfully angry at first, but then things got strange. The couple explained to Sy that they were Muslim, that the wife was barren, and that their religion made provisions for a man to have multiple wives for childbearing purposes.

The couple invited Sy to be a part of the family and raise her daughter as a second wife to this man. Shocked and confused, Sy called her mom, who was now remarried and living in Arizona. Sy's mom strongly disagreed with the arrangement and offered Sy a home out west. Sy thought it over, but she didn't want to keep her daughter from knowing her dad. Once Sy's daughter was born, she arranged for supervised visits with the father of her child. But after several disagreements with his wife on how to care for the baby, Sy decided the best thing for her daughter was one mom, no drama, and a new life in Arizona.

As soon as the two reunited, Sy's mom noticed a maturity in her daughter, and Sy saw a softening in her mother. They made amends, and their relationship grew strong. With her mom and stepdad's encouragement and help with childcare, Sy picked up extra work hours to retire her remaining loans so she could start back up with school. As quickly as she could afford it, Sy would take one community college class at a time in preparation for her nursing degree. She had her eye on the prize, and she was determined to get there no matter what.

Sy kept in touch with an old friend from Ohio, and they began a long-distance relationship. At Sy's invitation, he eventually moved to Arizona to start a new life with Sy and her daughter. They were happy together, and both pitched in to care for the expenses, the home, and Sy's child. With her CNA license, Sy was working at the local hospital in the ER. The hospital was contributing tuition funds to her BSN degree in exchange for her continued employment post-graduation.

Things finally seemed to be falling into place. But as Sy was about to begin her first block of the nursing program, she found out she was again pregnant. Sy took the news in stride. She had worked full-time during her last pregnancy, got her CNA license… she even lived in her car for a while. This timing wasn't ideal, but she had four semesters left and she was not about to slow down. Besides, now she had a partner who had her back.

A year later, Sy was a new mom, two semesters away from graduating and trying desperately to ignore the warning signs that trouble lay ahead. Her partner, she now realized, was an alcoholic. The patience and excuses she had once extended to him were now spent. She was beyond exhausted, and he was only adding to her load. The moment of decision came at 3:00 a.m. when after a long night working the ER, Sy came home to find her partner sprawled out on the porch, eyes wide open and fully unconscious. When the paramedics arrived, he was near death.

Putting the pieces together, Sy learned that he had consumed a life-threatening amount of alcohol while the children were in his care.

Addiction ran in his family. Alcoholism had claimed the lives of both his father and, more recently, his sister. She loved him and wanted to help him, but she just didn't have the capacity to take care of one more, and he had no interest in changing his ways. She reluctantly ended the relationship, and he returned to Ohio.

Sy tackled the first of her two remaining semesters with a heavy heart. She missed her partner and often wondered if she did the right thing by ending the relationship. Her mom and stepdad were helping with the kids, her brother was even pitching in, but she was lonely, over- worked, and losing hope. Then one day, on her way to work, her car broke down. This seemed to be her life, one challenge after another. Was the world going to always be against her? As she was figuring out what to do about her car, her phone rang. The woman on the other end of the line informed Sy that she had been accepted for the Helping Hands for Single Moms (HHFSM) scholarship.

Sy was caught off-guard. She tried to remember when she filled out the application and what this scholarship entailed. As the conversation went on, Sy decided to share what had happened that day. The director, Layla, listened, empathized, and let Sy know that part of the scholarship included car care. Sy was not a churchgoer, but she was a praying woman. Sy knew without a doubt that this phone call was God telling her, "I've got you. You're going to be alright."

Sy would hang on to those words, and her new relationship with the people at HHFSM, as she faced her last year.

The final semester was underway. The graduation date was set. In a few short months, Sy would have her BSN. As she drove the familiar route to work one January morning, a man stepped off the sidewalk and into oncoming traffic. Despite her split-second efforts, Sy could not avoid him and struck him with her car. The man was rushed to the ER but did not survive. The accident was determined to be the fault of the pedestrian, but Sy's heart was broken all the same. As the days wore on and grief threatened to envelop her, Sy fought to put her feelings aside. She couldn't ruminate on what had just happened. She had too much to accomplish in this short amount of time, so she told herself she could deal with her emotions once she finished her degree.

Five days later, while Sy was in class and the kids were at school, she got a phone call that her apartment was on fire. Sy and her children were grateful to be safely away, but they lost everything. The landlord told Sy that she was financially responsible for the damages and that he would sue. No one knew how or why the fire started, and Sy struggled to prove she had nothing to do with it.

She had studied medicine, not law. HHFSM got word of the events of Sy's week and stepped in to help. Layla brought Sy gift cards to help replace clothes, food, and other necessities that had been lost in the fire. An emergency fund check was delivered to cover the move-in costs of a new place to live, although Sy later returned the check to HHFSM after deciding to stay with her mom and stepdad while she finished school. Sy figured someone else could probably use the funds as there was this new virus going around that was causing businesses to shut down and people to be laid off from their jobs.

Graduation day finally arrived, even if it was not how anyone had envisioned it. COVID-19 had made its way across the country, and public gatherings everywhere were being canceled in an attempt to slow the spread of the virus. But Sy still celebrated. She had made it.

She had finally earned her nursing degree. She begins work towards her next goal, her Nurse Practitioner's license, in the new year.

"How did I get through it all? School and the kids. I was so close, I had to just keep going. I knew my problems would still be there when school was done. I also learned that life isn't meant to be lived alone. Encouragement from others is just what you need to get through the hard times because you can't speak encouragement to yourself. Others can remind you of the truth. Your challenges are things you are going through, but they do not define who you are. In other words, your problems are not your identity. They're just a part of your testimony."

FROM THE FOUNDERS

Dear Reader,

Common among these stories is Helping Hands for Single Moms partnering with single mom college student families on their path to success. As an organization, we are honored to have come alongside and provided a helping hand when their journeys were most difficult.

Helping Hands for Single Moms was founded in 2002 as a grassroots nonprofit in Phoenix, Arizona, whose mission is assisting low-income single mom families while the mother attains a postsecondary education, financial independence, and a positive family legacy. We discovered a unique role in the community as the only nonprofit completely dedicated to low-income single mom college students by providing a specific suite of wrap-around services designed to increase their likelihood of graduating.

A single mother's pursuit of a college education is a sure pathway to family stability, increased employment, financial security, and future advancement. However, single moms face incredible challenges as they attempt to work, attend college, and raise children. According to the Institute for Women's Policy Research, only 8 percent of single mothers who start college earn an associate or bachelor's degree within six years. We sought to improve that number dramatically.

Typically, "success" is measured by how many underserved single mom families receive minimal benefits to temporarily stay afloat, yet nothing ultimately changes. Their children grow up becoming another generation needing government and other support just to survive.

Our mission is inspired by our vision to end generational poverty. By helping single mothers become financially independent contributors to the community, they set a model for their children that breaks the cycle of poverty resulting in a multigenerational return on investment. We want to move families from surviving to thriving!

Strategic planning for our launch was facilitated through a 3-year pilot project with Arizona State University's Partnership for Community Development, who assisted in research and program evaluation. During that time, we used focus groups and other means to learn the unique challenges mothers faced as single mom college students.

In 2004, we completed the pilot project, and after years of fine-tuning we now provide the following suite of services:

- AAA services
- Budget management
- Car repairs
- Carpet cleaning
- Emergency support
- Family outings
- Haircut and style for mom
- Holiday gifts
- Legal counsel
- Life skills training
- Limited dental, medical, and eye care for mom
- Mentoring and coaching for mom
- Monthly stipend
- Professional counseling
- Single Mom College Community
- Tax preparation assistance

- Tech assistance for computers and software
- Textbook purchase assistance

Our Single Mom College Community focuses on personal and professional development as single moms learn life skills such as money management, resume writing, interview preparation, proper attire, and other competencies.

Single moms often feel alone, so time with peers, mentoring, and encouragement are vital towards their success. Meetings occur at least six times per year over a shared meal with subject matter experts presenting. The value of these meetings towards graduation and post-graduation success are priceless.

The services provided to our single mom families are delivered by community businesses, academic institutions, churches, professional sports clubs, civic organizations, and individuals. They appreciate the culture of success, exponential return on investment, and the value of "helping those who help themselves."

A 2016 study by "College Success Arizona" determined that a college degree is worth over $660,000 to the state of Arizona over a worker's lifetime. This amount included taxes paid, community services not needed, and the financial value of their skills. In Phoenix, our graduates and current students are on track to contribute over $250 million to the Arizona economy.

Educate the Mom – Educate the Family

We measure our program's success through the metrics of graduation, employment, and earnings. The outcomes have been fantastic:

- Near 80% graduate college.
- Most are employed immediately upon graduation.
- Initial earnings over $55,000/year, plus benefits.

As an organization, we have kept pace with the changing job market. In 2009, we responded to the growing demand for nurses by creating a nursing orientation to our program, including nurse mentors, discussions about the field of healthcare, preparation for the National Council Licensure Examination (NCLEX), and connecting graduates with job placement.

As a result, we have placed near 200 nursing graduates into the workforce, with nursing students now comprising many of our scholarships. Following graduation, they are placed to serve their communities with thousands of patients cared for through the recent Covid pandemic.

Likewise, in response to the fast-growing information technology (IT) sector of the job market, our newest Phoenix initiative is an IT program for single moms at Glendale Community College.

None of this would have been possible without support from the many private foundations and community partners along the way, including but not limited to:

- Arizona Cardinals Charities
- BHHS Legacy Foundation
- Blue Cross Blue Shield of Arizona
- Eddie Johnson & Friends
- Ibis Foundation of Arizona
- Phoenix Suns Charities
- Neighborhood of Automotive Repair Professionals (NARPRO)
- Southwest Airlines
- Valley of the Sun United Way

In 2014 we were introduced to former NBA great, Eddie Johnson. That opportunity and ensuing community partnership sparked the creation of our annual fundraising event, Eddie Johnson & Friends.

Thanks to our supporters we have delivered over $6 million in scholarships and services to over 1,400 individuals, including the single moms and their children. With about 400 total single mom families, either graduated or currently in our program, we are now seeing second-generation outcomes as children follow mom's example of graduating college – thus breaking the cycle of poverty!

Helping Hands for Single Moms has received significant recognition winning multiple awards, including:

- The esteemed "Judges Choice" award by KAET - TV Channel 8 for the non-profit that demonstrated "original and extraordinary effort," a notable honor that considered the work of 130 Arizona non-profits (2008)
- Statewide award recognition by the Arizona Commission for Post- secondary Education as an educational leader assisting single mom college students (2009);
- Our successful nomination for the Phoenix Business Journal's "Heart of Business" award for NARPRO (Neighborhood Auto-Professionals) for services to Helping Hands for Single Mom cli- ents (2011);
- Chris received the Arizona Education Champion award presented by the Arizona Commission for Postsecondary Education (2015).

Ralph Joins Fight to End Poverty

Ralph's involvement with Helping Hands for Single Moms Phoenix began in 2006 following his relocation from Bellevue, Washington. He quickly went from donor to Board member to Board President and was intimately involved in the growth of the Phoenix organization.

The idea to launch Helping Hands for Single Moms Dallas came on the heels of Ralph's relocation to Dallas, Texas. It took over three years to build public awareness, form community partnerships, establish the organizational structure, including the Dallas Board, and secure enough funding to launch.

Community partnerships provide essential services enabling us to multiply each dollar received. As an example, when our moms need auto repairs, we have an agreement with Firestone Auto Care service centers where we pay for necessary auto parts, and Firestone provides free labor. Given the uncertain timing of vehicle breakdowns, this is an urgent need in most cases, especially for a single mom college student family relying on a sole vehicle and individual for transportation. We facilitate the process for an efficient and quality outcome.

In 2019 the Dallas organization completed its first full year thanks to donations from the Dallas Mavericks Foundation, the Ryan Foundation, and others. We finished the year with a dozen single mom college student families in our program and celebrated our first graduate, Morgan, with a Bachelor of Science in Kinesiology from the University of Texas at Arlington. She is currently employed in her field of study and considering becoming a Physical Therapist.

In 2020 as a new startup organization, we faced significant Covid headwinds, but our moms and the organization persevered. We had four graduates, each with an Associate Degree in Nursing. This group encompasses dean's list recipients, including one who served as President of Collin College's Student Nursing Association. Most are continuing their education towards a Bachelor of Science in Nursing as they assist in the fight against Covid.

In 2021 we have eight single-mom college students and are adding another dozen this fall to end the year with twenty single mom families in the program.

Ralph received national recognition by winning the Catalyst Award presented by the Invest in Others Foundation. Invest in Others recognizes individual financial advisors and firms that are making a difference by donating their time and money to causes they care about. https://www.investinothers.org/finalists/.

Nominations are based on an advisor's leadership, dedication, contribution, inspiration, and impact on a nonprofit and the community it serves.

Ways to Provide Support

Throughout our twenty-year history, we have remained consistent in our vision and mission. We encourage you to join Dallas and Phoenix in our fight to end generational poverty by assisting low-income single mom college student families attain financial independence.

You may contribute to Dallas or Phoenix on our website www.HelpingHandsForSingleMoms.org. We also have planned giving opportunities for those who want to see their charitable donations have an impact for generations to come. Gifts include:

- Cash or checks
- Appreciated securities
- Stocks, bonds, mutual funds, exchange traded funds
- Donor-advised funds
- IRA qualified charitable distributions
- Land, properties on land (homes, buildings), along with property rights associated with the land

We also accept in-kind donations, so if your organization would like to support us, we would love to hear from you. This includes other nonprofits who have established services that would benefit our clients as well.

Community partnerships may be structured to provide ongoing in-kind support, which we would collaborate to define and structure.

Dallas and Phoenix have contact information available through the website to answer questions, share ideas, and facilitate donations.

www.HelpingHandsForSingleMoms.org.

Thank you,

Ralph Ujano and Chris Coffman

Ralph Ujano, Jr.

ABOUT RALPH UJANO, JR

R alph has been married to his wife, Julie, for 25 years and they have three children.

Ralph and Julie grew up in low-income situations and experienced its hardships. Being a "wrong side of the tracks" child is a challenge, and coming home to an empty house as a latch key kid everyday only made it worse. They observed and felt their parents' financial struggles.

On the paternal side of his family, Ralph has numerous cousins and is the only one who graduated college. Like our single moms, he envisioned a college education as vital towards his future, persevered through adversity, and now does everything he can to give others an opportunity to succeed.

Ralph and Julie had their first child before marriage and struggled apart for most of five years. Even though they were mutually involved they could see how a single mom situation would be extremely difficult. This gave them an appreciation of the challenges faced by single moms and how amazing they are at rising above their circumstances with just a bit of assistance.

Ralph spent over 30 years in the financial services and consulting industries, including C-suite positions where he was a central part of organically growing a single Registered Investment Advisory (RIA) office to twenty-two offices nationwide, becoming one of the largest RIA firms in the country. In 2017 Ralph started his own RIA firm specializing in multi-generational wealth management planning. He still dedicates a significant amount of time to community service.

Throughout their marriage, Ralph and Julie have lived in four states. In each location, they have been involved in numerous church and charitable activities. Upon arriving in Phoenix, Arizona in 2006, they were introduced to Helping Hands for Single Moms.

In the first meeting with Helping Hands for Single Moms Phoenix founder, Chris Coffman, he explained that their strategic organization model to end generational poverty started with a "teach a man to fish" approach ensuring the success of the single mom college student, as it would lead to the success of her children, and ultimately future generations. Multigenerational thinking and the incredible return on investment it produces is something Ralph understood well from a financial planning perspective and from his own life experience.

Following those conversations, Ralph and Julie attended a couple of the "meet the moms" events and were impressed with the stories of single-mom college students overcoming incredible odds to improve their family situation. They immediately knew this is where they were meant to serve and have continued that passion in their relocation to North Texas by launching Helping Hands for Single Moms Dallas.

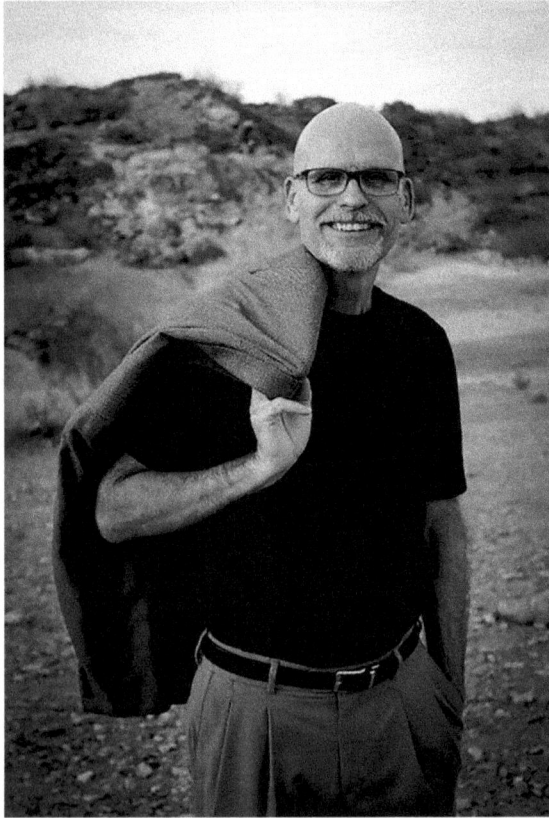

Chris Coffman

ABOUT CHRIS COFFMAN

C hris has been married to his wife, Kim, for forty-six years. They have four children and six grandchildren.

In 2000, after serving as a minister for twenty years, God began to direct Chris's heart into the community. As a result, Chris was the visionary and driving force behind the development of three major projects. The first was "El Amor De Cristo," a seventeen home Habitat for Humanity subdivision built solely by churches. The second project was Community Builders – a coalition of six Northwest Valley churches that provided quarterly service projects to assist the city of El Mirage. The third project – the one that fully captured Chris's heart – was Helping Hands for Single Moms.

Since its launch in 2002, Helping Hands for Single Moms has provided over $6 million in scholarships and supportive services to hundreds of low-income single-mom college student families.

In 2015, Chris was named "Educator of the Year" by the Arizona Commission for Postsecondary Education and in 2011 received a Golden Rule award from the Arizona Interfaith Movement. In 2008, Helping Hands for Single Moms received the "Judges Choice" award at the KAET Channel Eight "Be More" awards. Helping Hands for Single Moms was recognized as the top program for "originality and extra-ordinary effort" out of 130 statewide nonprofits.

Following Ralph's relocation to Dallas, Texas, Chris and Ralph were able to team up again as he assisted in launching Helping Hands for Single Moms Dallas.

Susan

ABOUT THE AUTHOR

Susan is a freelance writer with over 30 years of experience in marketing and advertising. She spent the early part of her career at various agencies writing for print, radio, and video media.

Transitioning into her freelance career, Susan was afforded the flexibility to raise three amazing children with her husband while creating content for various small businesses and non-profits. Today, she operates her writing and video production projects under the corporate name of Sweet Media, LLC.

Susan and her husband, Jon, were introduced to Helping Hands for Single Moms through Joanne Grady, friend, and former program director. They have actively supported the organization for over ten years - Jon serving a term on the board, and Susan volunteering her time writing newsletters. They have witnessed firsthand the impact an education and a solid support system have on lifting an impoverished single mom out of her circumstances. These women gain new hope, uncover hidden strength, and *they* become the role models that inspire their children. The lessons these women learn far exceed their education, and the benefits permanently impact the lives around them.

Susan is humbled to be a part of the project, *Heroes in Our Midst*. Her desire is to encourage every mother, single or otherwise, to press on through personal adversity for the sake of her children. Susan's hope is that she would do justice through the written word to these moms who so bravely lived their stories. And her prayer is that she would accurately share the work God began through his servant, Chris Coffman.

ACKNOWLEDGEMENTS

Heroes in Our Midst would have never been published without the following partners. Much thanks to:

- **Our eight moms** who transparently and courageously shared their stories.
- **Susan Sweet** for her many hours of interviewing the women and turning her notes into life-changing accounts.
- **Jim Aubele** who designed the cover and provided final edits.
- **Delta Emerson** whose community introductions and encouragement were an essential part of launching in Dallas.
- **Harrison Barnes and his mother Shirley** for taking part in our inaugural Dallas "My Mom My Hero" award.
- **Becky Norwood** from SpotlightPublishing.Pro who was fantastic to work with.
- **God**, who knew the need and inspired action to create Helping Hands for Single Moms.

Thank you!

If you were impressed with what you read, we invite you to leave a review at one of the online book retailers – reviews make such a difference for the book's visibility.

If you would like to offer support to Helping Hands for Single Moms please reach out via our website:

www.HelpingHandsForSingleMoms.org

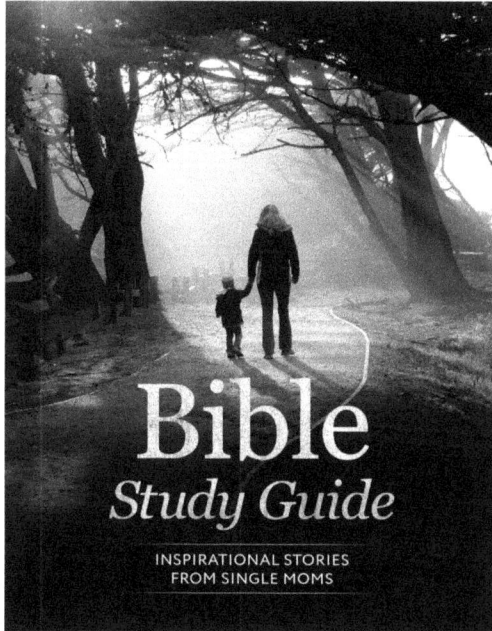

Download Our FREE
Companion Bible Study Guide
https://helpinghandsforsinglemoms.org/dallas/heroes-in-our-midst

www.ingramcontent.com/pod-product-compliance
Lightning Source LLC
Chambersburg PA
CBHW070640030426
42337CB00020B/4093